Ahead of My Time

...from the Streets to the Stages

Albert 'Infinite' Carrasco

inner child press, ltd.

Credits

Author

Albert Carrasco

Editor

hülya n. yılmaz, Ph.D.

Cover Graphics & Design

William S. Peters Sr.
inner child press, ltd.

~ * ~

Disclaimer from the Editing Department

In order to maintain the poet's colorful and authentic voice, this publication has not undergone the full standard scrutiny of editing. Please take time to indulge the author for his own creativity and aspirations to convey the uniqueness of his word art.

hülya n. yılmaz, Ph.D.,
Director of Editing Services

General Information

Ahead of My Time . . .
from the Streets to the Stages

Albert 'Infinite' Carrasco

1st Edition: 2021

This Publishing is protected under Copyright Law as a "Collection". All rights for all submissions are retained by the individual author and/or artist. No part of this Publishing may be reproduced, transferred in any manner without the prior **WRITTEN CONSENT** of the "Material Owner" or its Representative, Inner Child Press, Ltd. Any such violation infringes upon the Creative and Intellectual Property of the Owner pursuant to International and Federal Copyright Law. Any queries pertaining to this "Collection" should be addressed to Publisher of Record.

Publisher Information:

Inner Child Press
innerchildpress@gmail.com
www.innerchildpress.com

This Collection is protected under U.S. and International Copyright Laws

Copyright © 2021: Albert Carrasco

ISBN-13: 978-1-952081-44-6

$ 24.95

Dedication

This book is dedicated to all my supporters. Without you guys, none of this would be possible. I thank you with all my heart.

I would like to give a special "thank you" to Irene MTK for giving me my first feature shot in Harlem. I'll always remember that.

Mr. William S. Peters, Sr., I thank you for helping me share my visions.

Infinite the Poet 2021

Table of Contents

Preface — xiii
a few words from Jamie Bond — xv
a few words from Tammy Jones — xvii

The Poetry

Ahead of My Time	3
The Infinite Poet	5
A Soldier	7
Brainstorm 1	9
Brainstorm 2	11
My Arrival	13
Guns	14
A Love Jones	16
The Slums	18
Speed	20
The Urban Armarian	22
The Trap	24
The Grind	26
Infinite Tut	27
When I Talk	29
Raised by a Woman	31
Silent 'Til I Speak	33
Lost	34
War Scars	36
I Remember	38

Table of Contents... *continued*

It's So Easy	40
Vintage Castle Hill	42
I Am a Storyteller	43
Urban Psalms	45
Criminal Courts	47
My Silent Entourage	48
In the Beginning	49
In My Genes	52
Puerto Rican Sosa	54
Pusher	55
0-100	56
Why Now?	58
Trap Life Narration	60
One More Time to See Them	62
Ready for the World	63
Fit In	65
Poverty's Home	67
Acapella	69
More Losses Than Gains	70
Time Paid Ransom	72
Writing	73
A Justifiable Suicide	75
A Living Legend	76
Code of the Streets, Part 1	78
Code of the Streets, Part 2	79
Code of the Streets, Part 3	80

Table of Contents ... *continued*

Split Personality	81
I Had a Dream	83
Titanium Bars	84
There's a Reason	85
Guardians	86
Hard Days	87
I'm from New York	88
Dreams	90
A Donor with Limitations	92
It's Showtime	93
The Urban Bar	94
Forgive Us	96
Mental Movies	97
No In-between	98
The Underdog	99
I'm from a Place	100
Vintage BX	101
Danger	102
The Worst Was the Best	103
Urban Preaching	104
Grinding	106
Got It Bad	107
The Hustle	108
Lived and Learned	109
Had to Have It	111
Stage 8	113

Table of Contents ... *continued*

He Wanted In!	114
Lost Bail	115
Lucky	116
Phle-body-me	117
Summer Nights	118
Listen	119
You're Welcome	120
Tomorrow	121
My Home	122
Woodwind and Brass	123
Feel It in the Air	124
Mic Sex	125
A Bond	126
Baptism	128
Got Fat	129
Shine	131
We've Made It	132
Born - Day	133
Inferno	134
Construction / Demolition	136
My Ensemble	138
Everyday Life	139
About That Life	141
Scorned Consequences	143
Healthy in Heaven	144
A Poet Since 1984	145

Table of Contents ... *continued*

Guidance	147
Money	149
My Scroll	151
Infinite Teachings	152
I Thank God for My Hood	153
Shows	155
Word Player	157
Armageddon	159
Chosen	160
No Longer Here	161
Questions	162
A Father-and-Son Story	164
The Way I Grew Up	166
The Last Soldier of Poverty	168
The Lyrical Dealer	170
Infinite Poetry	172
Time Flew	175
Money-Hungry	177
Realness	178
Street Wars	180
The Power to Speak	182
Lyrical Deterrent	184
Scars	185
Urban Poetry Is My Life	186
A Hit-Man	187

Table of Contents ... *continued*

Shootout	189
The Hustler's Sons	191
Concrete Imagery	193
The Devil Had Me	194
Russian Roulette	196
Bipolar	197
Lost Boy	198
When and How?	200
Fossil-Fueled	201
A Diamond in the Ruff	202
I Am Living Proof of Change	204
His-story Repeats	206
Shattered Dreams	208
Self-destructive Adolescence	210
Mother and Son	212
Judgment Day	215
Man, Near Death . . .	217
A Gallery of Pictures	**219**
Epilogue	**239**
about the Author	241

Preface

Ahead of My Time . . . from the Streets to the Stages was put together like a puzzle. It is pieces of my life. Every poem has meaning and its purpose is to deliver knowledge. A mixture of Ebonics and Layman's is what I use for my form of urban expression. Sharing my journey in life is my method to saving other lives. I lived a harsh life and learned harsh lessons. Poverty led to the streets. In inner cities, doing so is almost tradition. My friends and i became the newest faces caught up in the traditional system of drugs, guns, fast money, jail and death. It rained, then the sun shone, then there was a torrential down pour of pain. I hope you the reader find value in my words that characterize my experiences. Perhaps together we can make a difference.

a few words from Jamie Bond

When you first meet Infinite the Poet, he comes across as laid back and unassuming. He is far from loud or boisterous, and he has the air of a 'bosses' boss'. Simply stated, this handsome hustler emulates what he gives . . . respect.

If you walk into an open mic, Albert Carrasco is not the poet in the back of the room; he is the one diagonal to the entrance or exit. He always seems positioned with a visual of the entire room. Now, by the time the event begins, he is engaged in the entire process leaning forward, elbows on thighs, hands clasped, and he is intently watching, listening, processing and studying. He is poised, ready to get it in. Once he is on stage, you feel the souls of the street soldiers he has bought up there with him as he takes full accountability and shares his pain and regrets . . . paying homage to the memoirs, biographies and eulogies of the fallen.

Can a hustler have PTSD and survivor's guilt from being out there and seeing so much? The answer is yes! There is no counseling if you survived the last episode, you're back out in the street ten toes to the ground, constantly tightening your circle, dealing with the paranoia of being snitched on or living like it's your last moment is 'bout to become next.

Back in my day, parents had a handbook by Dr. Spock on how to raise their children, and by the time I had kids, there was what to expect when you're expecting. My kids now have one of the most highly anticipated publications of his 2nd book which is a prelude to *Infinite Poetry*.

And now, ladies and gentlemen, 'Infinite the Poet's 2nd book, entitled *From the Streets to the Stages*, takes you from the street through stages spytin' his life on stages. This volume should be in every clergymen's, teacher's, child's and parent's hands.

If you're looking for purple unicorns and some 'poor me'-story, you'll be disappointed because this isn't a "scared straight" type program and it's far from a glimpse into how to cook crack and make it glitter. *From the Streets to the Stages* is not another 'I was a pimp dating a stripper back then' kinda book. Nope! As a matter of fact, have you ever been privy to seeing the playbook to your favorite sports team before the game? That's what this book is. It's an autobiography of all raw, uncut truth that lets you see yourself and loved ones in its lifestyle with hopes of a 'turnaround' from the attraction, the hooks and the latches, the behaviors, the lack of saviors, the damage, the pain and the risks . . .

Infinite's books feel like intense short stories ready for a Hollywood mini-series. You won't regret your purchase and you'll definitely learn from his shared insights. This collection makes reality shows look like lampoon skits . . . that shit's not real fams; Infinite the Poet's *From the Streets to the Stages* is!

Buy it, blog it, read it, gift it, tweet it, take a selfie, hashtag it, tag ppl, whatever you've got to do to get this book in the hands of the real ppl do that!

Jamie Bond
Published Author

a few words from Tammy Jones

Al Carrasco, AKA Infinite the Poet is the heart of a lion. Hear his roar of truth explode through his pen to the stage. His books need to be texts used in high school and colleges because he writes out an education most will never understand; and if death isn't an outcome, it could be jail if you are lucky to brag being a survivor. His story is compelling, believable and the honest truth about life on the edge. He lived it. He loved, lost and survived. He is the last man standing and is a legend. He lost many friends at young ages, and has seen their children grow up to adulthood.

Infinite the Poet is a role model for many. Al is a nice humble guy who supports poetry and friends, and he is an ultimate entertainer when his hand touches a mic. He definitely lives for his craft and is one of the few I know, who for the length of time that I have known him, will post a new piece each day. His first book, *Infinite Poetry*, was published in 2011. I only expect greatness from anything he does. Infinite the Poet does not travel light and you will never know who may be coming when you invite him to an event. His presence is heavily affiliated with heavyweights, and sometimes you may catch this spoken word artist rapping. I wish Al the best on his book and can't wait to see it released because I am ready to get my copy of *From the Streets to the Stages*.

Tammy Jones

Published Author
Hip Hope Productions
Hip Hope Publishing

The Poetry

Ahead of My Time . . . from the Streets to the Stages

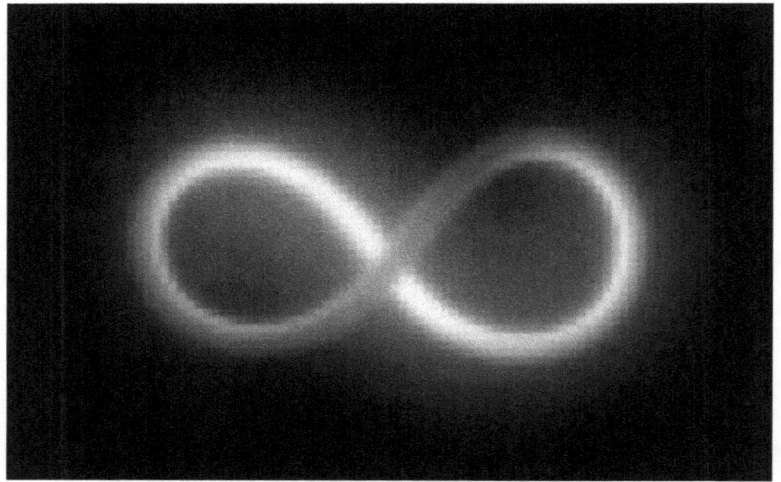

Ahead of My Time

I'm ahead of my time as a lyricist. Pardon me, but can somebody tell me what year this is? I'm going to start writing and practice reciting somewhere at higher elevation for stamina, so I don't get winded when I deliver education in urban areas.

Like jay as a rapper, I'm the ghetto poetic Magna carter. I graduated the school of hard knock, magnum cum laude. Infinite's profession is a professor of slum life oppression.

I was a kid genius with that igneous eina melted like magma in momma's coffee pot formed lava; when cooled, it returned to stone, then it broke homes, my sentiments go out to all the young revolutionaries that morphed into sedimentary trying to get away from poverty and that are now marked by marble metaphoric for dealing with rock.

My mind was in a comatose state for a prolonged period of time, my body was moving blind . . . I have awoken, my third eye is now open and I let it shine. I've been silenced too long; that's why I'm so verbose with spoken word on mics and poetry between blue bordered white lines.

My peoples and I were environmental products of circumstance. The difference between me and them is some sold their souls; I just danced with the devil under many pale moonlights, regressing as he had me in a trance lying, telling me with him I'll advance.

I stopped the duets and blocked his frequency from communicating with me; since then, eYe see clearly. In our last dance, I made him follow my footsteps as I spun, slid, moved up and down as I had him spell out blaspheme as he

mimicked the movements of my feet, then I laughed as I saw him spontaneously combust to the past.
I tap key's like a scheming, skimming transporter to save my sisters and brothers from discovering what I discovered, that's dreams of blowing up, they exploding like the challenger, unnatural disasters, street life massacres from claiming already owned housing acres as cookie bakers.

When I write, pay attention. I'm trying to preserve every mother's immaculate conception from crucifixion. I visit mosques to build and go to churches to drench myself and guzzle holy water, to spit this righteous wisdom to those trying to make a dollar from a quarter, to get out of squalor as block huggers and corner store hustlers.

The past can't be changed but the future can be saved. When I scribe about my life as a money slave, about the path that was paved from my forefathers' being enslaved to the same drug currency craze, my homies' names and their names will infinitely be in my heart . . . painfully engraved.

The Infinite Poet

The duty of the civilized man is to teach civilization. Read my bleeds and they'll become your salvation. Scribing about my life from the point of starvation to having surplus money, regardless of how much I spent to buy out connections to the end which was . . . Raids, Jail, evictions . . . Gunfights, viewings, last rights . . . Street life repercussions, is a deterrent from life in corrections or becoming a killer or a victim of a murder investigation.

I pray that none of y'all see drug money, because if you do, y'all won't leave it alone. It's addictive, it'll break homes and paint you ugly. Get rich quick schemes to possess the root of all evil changes individuals, especially the lucky ones that get to see lucrative residuals. You'll be ready to die, you'll be ready to let your team die. No one will say it but it is what it is. We just disguise the thought by saying we'll ride till death. I was trying get out of poverty by any means necessary. That was the same mindset of my friends . . . now, there's only a few left.

I'll go back to asking pancho for credit, back to wearing the same clothes daily and back to the everyday delicacy of eating rice with ketchup. If my friends could have a second chance at life if they're dug up. I've lost many. There's absolutely nothing I've done or had that was worth losing just one. I'll forever bear the burden of seeing parents crying for their sons, "daddy was and is a king". That's what I explain to bastard sons whose father lived by coke and dope and died by the gun. Life made me emotionally out of control when peeps are crying. I laugh when the world is cold.

I'm driven by trials and tribulations, by hurt, pain and other afflictions . . . It's something I'm used to for worshipping the almighty dollar like it was a religion. I have the genes of a hustler; the life was tradition. Knowledge, wisdom, understanding, three generations are at the highest level of extinction. If my words don't become saviors, I'm going to have to drop poetry, study law, pass the LSAT and become a public defender and moonlight as a funeral director so I can free y'all from supreme and criminal or put some respect on your name when family buries ya.

A Soldier

I knew I'll grow up to be a soldier . . . That day, when my mother came home and told me that they shot my father, I didn't cry. It hurt me badly internally. When she said he might be paralyzed forever, I was crushed. The rage and anger in me were already contemplating payback, revenge was a must. Momma, who did it? She knew but wouldn't let it be known. "You can't do nothing about it, albertito, but pray for daddy to come home."

Little did she know that every time she went into the shower, I went into dad's dresser, took the gat and posed in the mirror like a gangster with the shooter on my mind. As I'm actn like I'm pulln the trigger, they hurt my king . . . I'm prepared to be a baby face finster, a preteen killer. Those attempted murderers are so lucky. If I was older . . . they wouldn't have gotten that opportunity.

I would be up my big brothers' ass where he went. I wanted to go and let quality time pass . . . He's my idol, we're tight, we grew up in the hood so there were many times he had to fight. Well, we had to fight because I'll jump in and get some freebies in between his left and rights. Fair? Not when I'm here, if you hurt mine you have to hurt me . . . no fear.

"Take care of your mother and little brother by any means," before dad died, he made that clear. He must've saw me and big bro in him. Big bro was like his clone and when you saw me you saw Alfred like he went through reincarnation and out came a high yellow version. Not only did I come from the DNA of a hustler, I was passed on the makeup of a soldier. I grew up in the time of cooked coke as a crack baby, then a trap toddler, then a preteen manufacturer to a boss of a trademarked color . . .

My wrist got shackled, I got cuts, bruises and bullet holes following dad's orders . . . I just took it as the part of "any means necessary" to help my mother. Then I was hurt again . . . Because of my work, my big bro lived twelve years as a docket number. My king and idol is gone . . . I had to go harder. What can I do to take it a further than my forefathers? Sent word then enforced no pitchn on four corners, strong arm . . . Took it to another level, fear over love . . . power.

Started from the bottom, then rose to the top, had a family tree till branches started getting chopped. Like I said, I knew I'll be a soldier. I became one. Now, I mourn like one, went on rooftops to play taps for fallen Suns in the slums that were with me when we yelled jumbos jumbos to the point where it was upsetting to sit for hours, counting ones.

All I wanted was a little order, I hand to handed orders, gave orders, called in orders. I go to cemeteries and start from the first to die and end with the last . . . in that order . . . poor, rich to deceased . . . in that order, instead of tears coming out my eyes, I make the mic cry. When it's forced to listen, then I amplify the pain of an urban . . . soldier.

Brainstorm 1

I brainstorm, I see thunder and lightning, I see clouds, it's raining letters. I place both hands upon my head to stop it from exploding. Too many words are forming. I grab the pen and inhale, exhale, then implosion.

This is the ink from within the thoughts.

A little ball moves around the paper effortlessly, like an ouija board; manifestations from deep in my cerebellum leak. I transform them verbally when I speak. I am a medium between pad and pen. Without me, this finely cut tree wouldn't have a connection with my poetic fruition. I speak reality and truth about harsh living conditions. I write with all the energy in me to shake the world. This super human information highway sends mail that shakes seismographs and Richter scales. You can feel tremors daily, because daily, I write memoirs about dope and crack fiends and crack and dope addicted babies in incubators, shaking, detoxing; at 1-day old, they're kicking what mommy and daddy used and sold.

I talk about the drug plague that came and terrorized. It's like cyanide, a slow suicide, a rapidly growing form of genocide. We're killing each other! Homicide. From the sack of our fathers, we walk this world as scum. Each one teach one, we taught each other how to deal with drugs and guns. This is life in the slums, a life introduced to our youths, that's the same life as their father who passed, that's why there's so many step dads trying to raise other men's blind sons, they've been running in the dark so long with negative momentum, it's hard to shift them to what's right, towards light, to immaculate conception of children without sin.

These kids you see mean mugging and hustling are the faces of jinn. The devil is a liar, and "eye" won't let him win. His plans will foil versus my verbal tesla coils.

I'm a poetic urban billboard, I'm scarred and tatted, I'm mobile literature, my presence paints pictures, my soul beholds ghetto scriptures, I am a dominate man. No, not ego. 1 2 3 fills my cerebral, All seven grams.

Lessons are squeezed through my diaphragm, airborne as wisdom to civilize the uncivilized man.

I spit protocol in the form of amoebas and protozoa, waterfalls, tidal waves, tsunami. This is a brainstorm from an urban spoken anomaly.

Brainstorm 2

When I go deep in the zone, I scroll through memories buried deep in dome.

I see the past flash pass as I choose which vision I'm going to hone in on.

Sunshine, joy, hurt, pain, love, hate or street education to make pupils dilate.

Once I pause that internal reel to reel my mind and pen connects to write scriptures, you can see like pictures.

You'll get emotional, I'll make you feel like I feel.

Sunshine . . . my days were bright before dad walked to the light. Joy . . . after dad died, I found a way to keep my pockets tight. Hurt . . . I lost many men during that plight. Pain . . . remembering those cold days and nights. Love . . . most of the ones I love rest in cemeteries after losing a life and death fight. Hate . . . is the feeling I have when I have to say bye to someone who'll infinitely be physically out of sight.

Let me build of that emotion . . . this part is education. Dealing with the streets, I've learnt lessons. Most of them ended with an assassination of a loved one. Then mom and dad sitting on sofas in front of a casket, distraught, surrounded with arrangements of flowers from friends, family and hustlers. Pictures of the deceased are all over, laptops with slide shows are on repeat, there's someone in all black in every seat; in the front, next to the box of tissues, there's a book to sign for "I love yous" and "thank yous", and wallet size funeral cards for you to keep. After a eulogy and prayers, there's a caddy hearse outside for the last ride of him who eternally sleeps.

My Arrival

The world awaited this urban poet, like we wait for the cure of aids. I have arrived, infinite the burning lemniscate. I got that project, ghetto, slum, drugs and guns fire in my third eye, it transforms thought into sound; so, I manifest flame on the game the life the get rich plight commissary and kites, the transferring of bundles on conjugals for five times the capital. I got the real-life gift like whoopi, I speak to those swayzes, then relay messages to mommy and wifey demis. Doctor Carrasco, I got a Ph.D., power to her dead people, the deceased talk to me and through me. I'm a ghost writer, a formaldehyde and embalming fluent reciter. I put my heart into this. When I attack, most just murmur. My ink spills bloody murder like a dead kid's screaming mother; horrific scriptures as I paint mental pictures of a life so sinister. I speak the reality a lot, know but don't address it verbally. Well, hell was my home. I'm not scared to preach, cause only god can judge me, and I know I'm being watched as I teach the juvys, adults too; the ones with kids and married, having relations with coke or heroin that's adultery, and this is infinite poetry!

Guns

I was infatuated with guns. I used to shoot in the air to hear the sound, and was fascinated with the ting ting ting ting . . . when the shells hit the ground. I loved the power it resonates. I would dismantle them just to study the inner mechanisms; put 'em back together, go to the roof and spit the entire clip. The flash, the sound, the shells . . . a mind-gasm. I would travel to the sickest spots, hottest blocks, with just me and my gun cocked safety on the off switch safely by my hip. You had to in these dangerous slums.

I saw the effects of slugs in flesh before I was facing death, five ripped through my father, one hit his spine, had him paralyzed in a wheelchair. I knew my dad's strength, he wasn't gonna continue to bathe on those adjustable white chairs. He fought and fought hard; from a wheelchair, he went to a walker, from a walker to crutches, crutches to a cane, to no help at all, he had a slight limp and never walked the same. Power . . . I saw what they did to my father. I had to push him in his manual chair, had to clear all debris from in front of him while he used that walker, held his hand when he was using that cane. I thought to myself . . .

When I grow up, I'm going to get me a gun, so I can protect my family from this sort of future pain. I interpreted hurt into anger, rage and revenge. What they did to dad, I wanted to do to others. I was mad! Fascination . . . my mind underwent evil saturation, disturbed visions watching my king go through rehabilitation had me carrying the highest grain ammunition, had my mother's crib stock piled with military munitions. At fifteen for them, I was already in Juvy detention; at sixteen, two slugs ripped through me, slugs ripped through all my friends' bodies except for one . . . a jagged edge knife went through his anatomy. I mention him cause he was the one that saved me. That brother used his body as cover and took one right next to his jugular.

A Love Jones

She was a seducing cougar, she said she loved me, I loved her. When peeps found out I was messing with her, they said it wouldn't last, that she would be my demise or that our relationship was just a phase that would hopefully pass fast. They say love is blind. Well, I wasn't lookn for nobody, she found me. We had a blind date, courtesy of an OG. From that first night out, I felt something in my heart. No matter what people say, I knew she was the one and that we'll never depart.

When I held her in my palm in public, I got dirty looks. I didn't care. I'll admit it, I was whooped. She sexed my mental lovely, she told me she was going to get me out of poverty. She said, "albertito, I need to tell you something." I said, "what?" She said, "I been around the block a few times. I need a pimp; I never had a monogamous relationship. Dudes sell me raw or burn me into igneous to profit off cookie chips."

It broke my heart to share her, I wanted her just to be mine. I was a youngen with an adult New York State of mind; so, it was fine with me . . . growing up poor, I learned to never deny the hungry, and dudes was hungry; so, I shared. I handed her to him and her . . . and they paid me, some bought it to make life better and some for euphoria. I'm going all out with this chick, the pockets from my dirty hand me down jeans is getting thick . . . I'm in the bricks, taking orders.

I'm floss'n, my homies are floss'n, valet park'n something German as we popped bubbly, party'n and bullshittn, toastn to a new found way of earn'n . . . that girl had us shin'n. On the fdr or the west side, you'll see us breezn. We looked like a metal snake . . . hazards blink'n, high beam'n, traffic weav'n, making every move simultaneously follow'n, whoever's leadn, headers and straight pipes muffled the sounds of sunroof new gat testn.

We all now live for this girl, she made us all believers . . . Al, whatever you do, don't ever leave her . . . I had no intentions. It got to a point, where I needed her to maintain a lifestyle. Since she's been around, all we've seen was good times . . . that was because we hadn't witnessed a mother's scream, a father's anger, the sadness of sons and daughters because daddy or junior flatlined.

I was in love with a whore, a puta, a killer. Her name is co-ca-eina.

She used me and many friends of mine; now, I'm using her to lyrically blow people's mind. I was twelve in 84, the birth of cooked coke; so, you can call me a crack baby cause that same year, I started selln what fiends bassed or mixed with weed or in cigs to smoke. As a survivor of the trap . . . showing the young world the un-glamorized part of the game is how I'm giving back.

The Slums

Where I'm from in the slums, young sons dump dubs and pop bubbly in housing lobbies trying to make a million before they become teens; same goals, some on different teams, similar dreams, stack cream feeding thc, pills, boy and soft girl fiends. Live and try, or live to just die. It's in their genes to try. They're prepared to spill and leak blood to possess paper of pics of dead men and a pyramid eye.

Why? Because there's a slim chance they could get rich, might have to walk over corpse after corpse. They understand the lifestyle is a bitch; so, they go hard before eternally resting in a ditch. If you take something of theirs, they'll kill you, slow their money up. They'll kill you, if they're at rock bottom and you're at the top from rock climbing. They'll be plotting on killing you, when you have it all then find yourself with nothing left. There becomes a very thin line between life and death.

The game is hell without flame. It's a jungle, survival of the smartest and strongest like the food chain. Some will eat, some will sleep on hot tar and concrete in these New York streets. I know firsthand, the fat lady sang, guns banged, slugs ripped thru meat. It's all business when hustlers with burners meet.

I wish I could say this is fiction but this life is tradition to many families living under poverty-stricken conditions with brave-hearted children lacking direction. It's hard to direct them when they're out, trying to help heads of households fight eviction. They see a fast way to pay rent and possess materialism; so, they run wild picking up momentum until they're stopped by the system or redrum.

Albert 'Infinite the Poet' Carrasco

Once they see a few stacks, believe me when I say they're not looking back. It's pedal to the metal, full throttle in the dollar, dream like lotto in a low low drinkn momo, spinning on momos in something foreign, copped with blood pesos on the road to the riches before seeing COs or stiff in tuxedos with a line of family and friends taking turns to give forehead besos.

Speed

It's crazy how fast time passed. There must've been a turbo system attached to the earth to speed up its revolutions. It's as if life came with an unlimited NOS tank that had a sticky button.

Yesterday's come too quick; so, I broke night after night, sometimes days were 72 hours long. I was trying to be slick. Three days of hustling, popping momo, gutting, then filling sticks, shouting carver, Peter and foxx . . . My color in the bricks.

I remember asking to be put on, dudes looked at me funny and told me, "Shorty, be gone." I looked at them, like okay, okay it's gonna be paybacks. Got my first pack, made my first sale . . . "Shorty, let me get two jacks" . . . put my PC back, went back and got one plus copped one, since bomb one the climb begun. I rose, had to fight me a one d if ya didn't re before empty or if I found the spot closed. Poverty and NYC made a monster out of me. It wasn't safe to approach me or talk to me if it wasn't about currency, had a one-track mind, had to build up that trap of mine, hard or lines, white crime.

A lot of dudes was getting it, bellaco is just on another level, them cats that didn't put me on are feeling it, damn he came to us when he was a youngling, we shouldn't have knocked his hustle. Luckily, I held no grudges, when their well ran dry, I pulled up with the German purring, turned down the kardon, like here small fries, take this and hit me later pulled off playn ricky . . . Don't cry dry your eye, they'll be looking at me like . . . inf is one hell of a guy. I'm flipping weight like body builders, flipping truck tires, steakumms and TV dinners turned to chefs standing in front of me cooking T bones over fire. Poverty is a thing of the past, had to wear fatigues cause I needed the extra pockets to hold wads of cash.

My team, they're living the same, everyone is an MVP of the game, I shine, they shine, they shine, I shine, we all gained. We got bigger than anticipated, movements were sophisticated, plots were intricate, we thought we had it down to a science. Along with the hustle comes violence and massive homicides as causes of death on certificates, free all those with 80s and 90s dockets, they already paid for illegal profit, from the bottom we went to the top quick, now I ghost ride my whip sitting behind the cockpit, pushing the pedal to the metal trying to reach Mach infinite. The fast life, the ghetto Audubon, once-a-year killers went home with less slugs than they had in clips causing an urban eclipse . . . Another mother losing a son.

The Urban Armarian

The world is my scriptorium as I put these urban scripts together of poverty, drugs, prison and murder like a ghetto life armarian. I am a truthbrarian, a third eye optician for those that can't see through the facade with normal twenty twenty . . . I correct those visions. When I was young, I was that little boy looking at the hustlers' hustle, I saw all the happy times, all the smiling faces, I saw the bling swing as they jumped in Lincolns and caddy's and sped off like it's the races . . . I was poor; so, seeing this left me in awe . . . I wanted to be like them, so did all my friends.

Besides wishing for steady meals, we imagined ourselves with all the materialistic items we couldn't afford and wondered if we ever really possessed them, how would it would feel? That was the beginning, when the facade first started deceiving us. We're out in the streets with karate slippers and chancletas, shorts made out of cut jeans, white Ts or wife beaters in the summer. It was almost the same ensemble in winter, just add tube socks, the last pair of jeans we didn't cut and an over or undersized never fit right hand-me-down sweater telling ourselves . . . there's gotta be something better. Better to us was becoming those hustlers; so, we became those hustlers.

The ones that were living like stars are no longer out here. I found that odd, it was just a hidden part of the façade . . . but at this point, we didn't care . . . we were here! We was gettn high, partying and bullshitting while celebrating emancipation from our usual poor classification. Bottles are being popped, gems are being copped, springs on something fast were dropped, chips, heads ported and polished, we're living lavish off what we established. To others, like us then, this is the facade at its finest . . . wars, cases, trials, bails, bonds, retainers, body bags, coroners, weeping mothers, missing faces.

Those are the things that remained out of sight when we were looking at others in the lime light. We didn't see those hustlers going to court, we didn't see those hustlers burying their brothers, we didn't see all the mother weepers, all we saw was what was shown . . . that's the facade full-blown. Now I know where the hustlers before me went. They went to jail, they went back to god, some are lucky to have survived the subliminal and are lucky to be walkn the streets still hustln like me minus powdery material. When it comes to the hard knock life, I'm fluent. I speak about the facade to help others see right through it.

The Trap

All I thought about was the trap, when I laid my head to rest, I put the gat and pack under the pillow but left the vest on regardless if I was uncomfortable. As soon as I woke up, I reached for the mag, the zip lock bag, sparked an L . . . That's breakfast in hell, took out yesterday's profit from all my pockets, weighed ones on the beam and put the rest thru money machines, stashed everything except for twenty singles for hand-to-hand exchange change in my dirty jeans.

I walked into the bathroom to brush my teeth, took off the vest and sweaty wife b to wash the saltines and my ass, dried up dressed up vested up strapped back up gave mamma a kiss and grabbed the pack before I went back out to hit the ave. Money is always on my mind. I was on a twenty-four-hour grind, you could find me in front of the bellaco building or on the benches in the big park at any given time.

I was a binge hustler. At times, it was weeks or months since I saw my brothers and mother, time was consumed going round the bx advertising my color, looking for prices that were lower, dropping off and picking up scrilla. I pitched with pitchers . . . they say if you want something done right, do it yourself; so, I stood there showing them how to get that hard white off. I was an Indian that became a Chief . . . fuck a boss, bosses sit back and call shots . . . most of the time, without putting work in. I called and sent them. Got a death wish? Come at me and or my kin, and I'll assist suicide like kevorkian.

Nobody put a hand out to help my family. I was running around passing credit slips like bad checks in the bodega or one of the one hundred forty-four apartments in my building from the projects; so, I didn't want to hear shit about me doing wrong by selling narcotics. Poverty corrupted me, prison nor attempts on my life was gonna stop me from stackn currency. Infinite was a twelve-year-old pallbearer, then again four years after, then again and again . . . I carried a lot on my shoulders, family and soldiers, nothing was gonna stop me from pushing flinstone boulders, the worst thing I had to do was pull the plug on a brother. I said prayers then went back to get blasphemous paper . . .

All I thought about was the trap, when I laid my head to rest, I put the gat and pack under the pillow but left the vest on regardless if I was uncomfortable. As soon as I woke up, I reached for the mag, the zip lock bag, sparked an L . . . That's breakfast in hell, took out yesterday's profit from all my pockets, weighed ones on the beam and put the rest thru money machines, stashed everything except for twenty singles for hand-to-hand exchange change in my dirty jeans . . . that repetitive action made me lose more than I can ever gain, cash ruled everything around me . . . I felt the pain.

The Grind

When you're hustling and that hustle monopolizes your time and you can't be around like you used to/want to, some people will get all up in their feelings. "I aint fuckn with them, they think they're hollywood", or "they too busy for us." Listen . . . I'm talking for me and all grinders trying to better themselves. Opportunity doesn't come often for a lot of us. Some had it and lost it for not giving whatever it was 100 percent of their time or not knowing how to maintain it; some never had it but waited patiently to clutch onto that opportunity. So, by no means are they willing to let it go. When we see one, we go after it; no noun can come in between . . . we are focused on goals. If our time means so much to you . . . grind with us, support us most of all . . . try to understand us. There're people I know for years and family that haven't come to a show or purchased my book or the twenty plus I'm featured in . . . it's okay, there's no animosity . . . When we reach our goals, a lot of you will still prosper; so, don't get mad at our hustle.

Infinite Tut

I'm a ghetto pharaoh, a slum life monk that slept with the devil, no homo. I mean, we shared bunks while I was kid like a bid. They say, keep enemies close . . . he couldn't have been closer tempting me with fibs. He was the cause of me living blasphemous as well as the cause of crematory ash blowing in the wind like dust on the ave. Perdon, madre Mia, I didn't want to grow to be a felon repeater but I didn't want to be poor either. Death . . . wasn't scared to go to paradise and see my father, the system. The lifestyle comes with prison; went to jail and got shot but that didn't keep me from burning Pyrex pots to chop rocks then pack little sacks to put in zip locks as bundles to hustle on hot blocks, evading ghost narcotic cops and more intended, attempted or stray shots.

I thought I was going to die . . . every day; so, my duty was to party harder than yesterday, splurging profit from ye parlaying in spots where big boys played. I was a coke boy before the label. Inf was a misdemeanor in the kitchen transforming co-ca-eina or grinding and mixing boy at the table. I was large. At fifteen, I caught a gun charge. By sixteen, I saw how it looked to see a member of the crew get placed in a hefty bag as garbage. Since then, all I saw was destruction and all I heard was the sounds of violence from dealing with connections and selling pestilence. The chirping of birds was my alarm clock, I'd open my eyes and quickly reach under the pillow to grab my gat, jump out of bed and grab a pack, then run down to advertise my color caps on the block.

Feeding fiends was routine, because welfare increments wasn't helping to achieve the American dream, and I was a street dreamer like my father; he just morir soñando in that pursuit of the almighty dollar. His nightmare ended; so, I took his place, was moving at a faster pace . . . he always said I was his ace before I saw his death face. Número uno was cheffn powder to a paste, walking the strip with the blicky at my waist getting off that bass. The streets are all I knew; pops didn't make it but I'm trying to reach financial freedom like the last that blew.

He died, he died, homicide after homicide; urban genocide was the result of wishes of pushing foreign rides by pimping the white bride . . . she was a hooker, weak men and women got hooked on her, they abused but she was really the abuser . . . no BJs and lays, it was dimes, nickels and treys. She was the way sun rays shun through dark clouds changing pain rain to bright days . . . that's if you controlled her instead of becoming addicted to her. Ya know, looking for her love but short for a date, so you walk around with a cup begging for quarters to make a few dollars to splurge as they lust purge.

When I Talk

When I talk about drugs and guns, it's not to brag. If I wanted to brag, I'll just talk about all the good times . . . power, women, materialism, brown paper bags full of currency like grocery, and leave out the jail time and body bags to further corrupt those who think blasphemy is a religion.

I don't do this for fame. My life was televised for decades; so, sons, dads and grandfathers know my name. Three generations witnessed my run for ill-gotten gains. I either dealt with them or made them, shook ones from muzzle flash flame . . . when trying to inflict pain for violating rules of the game.

I'm not on the mic like 'look at me, look at me!' I grab it to recite urban scrolls like hear ye hear ye, better listen to me so you won't be another voice speaking to me through my Ph.D. That's the power to hear the dead . . . an earned hard knock degree.

Knowledge brings sight to blindness. Since I know the ledge, I spit righteous abyss so mothers don't have the embalming fluid taste on their lips after giving junior a final kiss.

These youngens need to stop anyway. They aren't built the way hustlers were back in the day. They be on their house jack ordering ye, on their cell phones bragging about gunplay and taking pics of guns, drugs and scrilla, throwing up signs dressed all in one color and posing like gangster social media killers.

Do y'all have a hustler license? Real bad boys move in silence. Why so loud? Why so flamboyant? I know, I know . . . ignorance. My people are still hungry and are ready to sacrifice to ball, they're sacrificing themselves for nothing at all, because before rising, they fall.

What dudes earn in a day nowadays makes them feel like a boss. What dudes make nowadays in a week is what was lost when the narcs rushed and we took a half hour off. No disrespect, but take it how ya want it. Y'all are in the street bussn and duckn shots twirln pyrex pots to make working man profit . . . It's not worth it.

Raised by a Woman

Infinite was raised by a wisdom. My old earth told me if I didn't have something nice to say, don't say it at all and never to volunteer information. This is why when I recite what I write, I have to keep it tight. She knows Al is her rebellious son, this time not listening will not have her knees with her hands clasped together, praying that I'll continue to evade murder. She overstands that I'm speaking about the bad freely to save urban sons with my Ebonics dialect-accented urban tongue.

I'm a hard knock valedictorian. No matter how long the next man's run is, next to me they'll always be salutatorians. I was always dealt the worst hand, been to hell and back. I earned bullet holes, a scabbed soul and scared heart along with a tan. I might sound like a hypocrite but I was ready to die at the same time it was a flatline for whoever tried, wasn't going out without a bang . . . My team either . . . guns rang . . . I lost most of the gang. The pain of losing them couldn't hurt harder, knowing that I wasn't there to save them when the fat lady sang.

Gats stood at my waist. I looked front, back, side to side, walking cautiously at a steady pace, hoping today is not the day I have to foil an attempt and catch a homicide case for myself or the remaining survivors from home base. So, we didn't live roofless; we lived ruthless. Living ruthless left youngens lifeless, witnessing close ones go through rigormortus is the reason why I leave blood traces on paper when my pen passes. Watching parents cry and yell on spots where JR fell makes me dig deep like JR's gravediggers when I nonfiction stories tell.

I hate seeing people I haven't seen in years and they ask for my peers. I say hate because it's going to be a long conversation as I give incarceration and death explanations. I relive it all as I crush the hearts of the people asking the questions, as I play back what my retinas recorded with third eye simulation. Quote the g.o.a.t, my words in repetition are rays of hope for Rey's and reinas caught up in the game of tress, pills, coke and dope. I was you. You don't want to be me. I have to look at names and the faces of my running mates, engraved on marble in Bronx bordered cemeteries. At times, I pass so much time staring I get escorted out by security. I hassle them but gain composure and leave. They know the love I have for my friends. I just go another day. I'm bred to be a brother's keeper. I had to train myself to understand that it's okay to leave because they can't die again.

Silent 'Til I Speak

I'm silent like that g under flat ruffled noodles, meat, cottage and mozzarella unless I'm spittn something laced or acapella. The bx is my two-time birth place; one was in 71 when I was pulled out of mom's c section, the second in 84, a crack baby being fed by multiple connections. I'm a Puerto Rican that bought Dominican cake to bake and have drawers stacked with Valencia, Asians imported china that had fiends holding up projects thinkn they're leaning like pisa. Every other NYCHA window had a portrait of a different color Mona Lisa, not blank stares . . . they're wondering how and when will they get out of there.

If it's not that, it's water pain dripping on windowpanes as they see junior and friends trying to make that happen by girl and boy hand to hand transactions. Gunshots, yells, sirens and screams of color advertising echo echo echo throughout the ghetto. Sales were made around cardboard and candle murals. We just threw one in the air or poured out beer, sayn a fast life psalm then . . . We'll see you when we get there after every finished bomb.

Had a club of hustlers like Larry; no thots just bosses of blocks. We grew up with each other from vial to slabs to loose rock, from derringer to Taurus to glocks to nickels dime dubs to playing dominoes with wrapped rectangles on marble tables before they're chopped. I miss my brothers, except for two . . . murder was the case that infinitely prevents me from seeing their face. The reality of the dream for me was experienced early, after it all I see it even clearer, I continue to be a blood writer and a mic bleeder. The only time I'll stop is through periods and breathers.

Lost

Driving through the hood late nights is bittersweet, bitter because death is the biggest reason there's no one roaming the street; sweet because the ones that didn't die got out safely and are living somewhere discreetly, traveling in the shadows secretly.

At any given time, there was somebody on the grind. I could always depend on finding a teammate whether it was early or late. The street was how we ate. We had shabby shelters but we lived in the trap trying to make a quarter turn into a dollar to see if life on the other side of the grass was greener after living instead a level above squatters.

It was clock work, like "happy days" . . . one o'clock two o'clock three o'clock . . . all around the clock there was sales of rock . . . it was work. Young felons did all-nighters, making sure brown bags didn't get swept by nycha. There was so much ammo on the strip like it was Garza. The lobby smelled like beef and broccoli. Godfathers, dudes passed L's gats and packs hiding the game from mothers and fathers. We ran from cops and let off shots at robbers . . . this was life. We lived for each other.

I'm gettn it, and so is my kin; we're infamously rich liv'n in hous'n. I see it in my head as if it was yesterday, every time I go around the way. Sometimes I pull up by the big park, park, spark, walk around and still bug out how everything went down. It's so real it feels fake, but the pain I feel when I'm there reminiscing of good times lets me know I'm not dreaming and it's all real . . . I'm wide awake.

I wish I can see . . . this is the sad part, many that lived bravehearted dearly departed; so, it's hard to say one name without mentioning another. So, I'll make it fair by saying, I wish I can see a brother walk out the lobby and give me tap, pull me close and fist-tap my back. I wish I can see my brothers sittn on the benches dug in like trenches. I wish I can call my brothers out the window . . . ayooo, skeeeyuuuuuu, see them and holla, lets goooo,

I do my circle, 635, the 60, the 40, back to the front of the bellaco building looking at 575, the boot and the 20. I start talking to myself . . . "Damn inf, what happened?" We promised to ride and die. So, they're in heaven, ghost riding phantoms. It's like having a Q and A during temporary insanity. If I stay there, y'all will never hear real life urban poetry, cause the ghetto griot will really go 730. I throw away the clip, chuck up deuces for my peoples and bounce Dolo . . . it should be a full vehicle

War Scars

I'm out here sporting war scars like they're tats if ya catch me with a wife b you'll see bullet holes and the names of a lot of dead men that got sent back. I'm a canvas of hurt and pain from the game of illegal gains . . . The streets are the artist. I ran the bx with drugs and guns before I was able to cum. I know cause I would beat off for hour and just have a boner. I'll get out the shower, melt Caine and soda to a gooey gum, then go out with arms that'll rip through stage one armor in the slums.

Inf reps the bx . . . hard body. I'm that boricua that's a lighter shade of brown with green eyes that made Spanish pañas proud of the way we moved pies in the east part of the boogie down. See, I'm from a time where not everybody with get rich quick dreams can hustle, violate a block, before you finish your first pack. You'll be laid out breathing in and out blowing blood bubbles.

I started from scratch with that kitchen recipe. A few tried, but nobody was fuckn with me. I quickly became a legend like bicicleta for having a hard yay flow like manteca. Real recognizes real. It's quite simple, if ya look into my eyes you'll see 100% . . . three numbers and a symbol. I'm so affiliated and I don't bang, met a lot of good men in the back of trucks on the chain gang. They got put on if they were bagged for the same thang. I was generous with the igneous. If they couldn't make bail, I made it for them; and on the way out of booking . . . on the road to riches to the riches and diamond rings, real men do real things is the song we sang.

Trapping was my life. That powder that glistens like diemonds carried my last name. Her first name is Caine. I was young and knew mamma would contest marriage; so, me and Coke eloped.

Albert 'Infinite the Poet' Carrasco

I was on the block like Ruben . . . a blade, guayabera and extra mags for the sauer to prevent hell's serenade, kept packs stashed in eye-view while keeping eyes on jake, creeping back and forth from up top from sound view. It was work. The hood was my lively hood.

Incarceration . . . slug penetration . . . burials and cremation . . . all came with the job. I got bagged, I got hit, along mothers and fathers . . . I sent day one sons back to god. I started alone and almost ended alone, had to retire before the last expired. It's crazy how I have till death loyalty. Whatever I do my remaining kin wants in; so, I removed negativity and move cautiously trying to build a positive empire in NYC.

I Remember

I remember rolling oowops in the bricks then jettn on the cross breezy to the west side to forty doo wops to take flix. Us spicks carried the stereotype but kept the Cadillac double parked with oowops and macs with machine shop aftermarket silencers and clips. Old school trey, eight blue and whites used to see us posing and taking puffs, but there was too many of us; so, instead of tryn to get a collar and get left with fully auto holes or Puerto Rican neck ties, they kept going straight. No man was gonna police us as we chased riches. If you saw how we lived without the streets, you knew we was serious.

I know the authorities couldn't understand how we organized crime when a lot of men couldn't read or write. It's because taking shifts young to feed long lines made schooling part time but made us hard knock geniuses. I went to school. I stood in stevo till eleventh grade, but when I got shot, the board of Ed said I have to go and that I couldn't return to any school in New York because they got information that I was helping poor people live out fantasies illegally like a ghetto mr. rourke.

It was ok though. I did self-schooling. I read dictionaries and encyclopedias. While the fresh hard was drying, I read and studied dad's 1-20 lessons, read the bible cause mom's a Christian. Nobody could say I was dumb or tell me I didn't have religion. Every morning, I went to kips bay to pump iron. I mixed brain and braun + the handed down power from my father to became a hood valedictorian. The blueprint was introduced and followed.

The regime was like a huge machine. The sprockets were members of the team. We ticked and clocked silently round the block like a Rolex . . . unless stick up kids or hit men came, then the guns will pop. Those dumb attempts rendered those stick-up kids and hit men useless. One hundred and forty+ apartments filled with three or more tenants but there's no witnesses! The building residents knew we never started nothing but at all cost they knew we would defend that business. If they went out after and picked up all the shells that was spent so forensics won't be able to lift prints and study flash holes, we would help pay rent and a few dollars for a later part of the month compra . . .

If you paid attention to the beginning, I said I remember. It's not like that any longer; hence, the past tense. The life for me is dead like my brothers, my street soldiers that returned to the essence in the pursuit of happiness, which meant the stacking of presidential paper . . . like my homies that got locked up in their twenties and will never again kiss their mother cause the feds push them farther and farther, to make visitations harder. How can a project, Mitchell lama and section eight mother afford a trip to show affection to her child in texarkana?

Some never got to physically see their sons and daughters cause they were already incarcerated when wifey reached ten centimeters. Now at twenty-five or thirty, these young men and women only know daddy through pictures, written scriptures and from survivors. Some of my friends' children get to see their deceased parent on a regular, thanks to technology and the ability to laser-engrave life-like faces on marble before being placed in cemeteries. Money, brains and brawn couldn't stop lifetime bids or lifetimes to mourn. I remember . . .

It's So Easy

In this spoken word game I done came up. It's been a decade and a half since my last re-up. Only if I knew when I was over the stove with a Pyrex whipn girl and soda in boiling water that I can get paid off the words I brew, I would've still had my crew. No one would ever see me. Where's Infinite? That dude is busy writing books for all his homies, that's the answer peeps would get when they asked bout me. Damn, why did they have to die? It's so easy . . . their story is the same as mine. I would've ghost-written till they were comfortable bleeding their own lines.

See I been spittn since the real summer jams, me and crazy Ill would rock for bam, but the gift got overshadowed by melting grams, running from the man and stackn pyramid eye paper with, the face of a dead man. Why rap when I had a trap? Why waste time playn with words when I can flip birds? Those were the thoughts running thru my head before the frequent ceremony of releasing doves for the dead. I could've saved them all. If I had honed in on my skills, we would've not needed drugs to ball. I would've not seen my homies on the floor like a fetal ball. I would've not seen blood on walls. I wouldn't have to explain to parents about the reason for nine-one-one calls . . .

Bellaco would've been a label instead of legends of the kitchen and table. We had an opportunity to be household names to households other than just the ones that sold doo-G and Caine. Sorry, I failed y'all my brothers. That's why I'm unapologetic when I grab a mic and release pain, when I expose the downside to the game, when I talk about how you'll lose more than you'll ever gain speeding blind in the fast lane. Inf spits straight nonfiction diction on the life of medicating with no prescriptions. I'm a flame thrower, cause I burned in supa nova, watching caskets go lower and lower.

Albert 'Infinite the Poet' Carrasco

There's a slug in me, bullet holes on me, I'm scarred . . . I have a coagulated anatomy. Cut me open, and scabs will drop out of me. I'm hurt beyond the senses. Why??? Because the way we went about riches lowered the numbers of family members when they did the census . . . it was senseless. That's why when it comes to saving the new generation, I'm relentless. I kissed the foreheads of day one homies frozen stiff and breathless.

Vintage Castle Hill

I walked out my apartment into Yellow pissy and tagged up elevators. I rode down, holding my nose figuring out what all the tags say. TV5, Zulu, TR nation, the "castle hill never ran, never will." That was always freshly thrown up caught my attention; sider beck presweet krs 1 are just a few graff artist always on rotation. I'll get to the lobby, walk through the park exit and see crazy mike and the garcia clan with pits locked, jawed on tree branches. The castle hill kings playn basketball. In the grass field, I'll see Hector and Raul Laboy setting up a game of hard ball; on the other side, nene and andy wash squashing and crushing anybody holding the football. I walk around to the front and see a young Ray Robles and the Camachos playing wiffle ball, and in the back, Juan Axle Bobby and Sandro were using the chalk strike zone for sponge ball. I'd play with the fellas till I got hungry. That's when I went across the street to Ralphy's truck, up the block to get mike's pizza or to lucky five and get the best roast beef and cheese ever, then come back to my building, sit on the cleanest abandoned car, eat and watch Edgar, Ralphy and Orlando doing gymnastic flips on old mattresses and listen to re-runs of all night long by the mary jane girls, ring my bell by Anita Ward and Stacy Latisaw's love on a two-way street courtesy of speakers on sills blaring out windows. Max was already and instrument playing along with breaking, Jorge was in the mix of groc making, el was head spinning and cheese was turtling. At the end of the day, I'll go upstairs, play, stop and rewind some tapes and lyric cram so I can come out at night and recite word for all the tracks played in the park jams.

I Am a Storyteller

Infinite . . . lived in a two-bedroom apartment with six heads in the jects. There wasn't a lot of room but there was lots of love. There wasn't a lot of money but we did have a big close-knit family. Momma fed us all. She's the head. I was little. I didn't really understand putting clothes on our back and food on the table was such a struggle . . . I realized that as I grew older . . . I saw her cash checks, pay bills and have nothing left over.

I remember hearing my father saying "take care of your mother" it was that time, I had to make life easier for this mother of mine. My big bro had a head start, he hit the streets pushing aside graff art. We couldn't settle for less. We have lion hearts. He's was in Audubon and Amsterdam with all the older cats; I stood in da bx with a hustln brat pack. We took over where big bros left off. From the bottom, we went to the top with hard from soft. We had to hide bombs, money and gats from our mothers as we went through the spectrum of vials with different colors.

When fiends want what they want, there's no holding them back . . . I'm telln moms, I'm working for security. They see me with her walking thru the hood and still ask . . . "Yo, AL, you good?" I need hard and nose candy. I'll mean, mug 'em so they get the hint that they have to wait so I can hit 'em. The entire squadron had that problem. Our parents weren't stupid. They were street smart living in hous'n. We went thru punishment, punches, slaps and flushed packs. They sent us to grandmothers and separated fathers but it was too late. The old "us" were goners. We are the new generation of block huggers.

Us ghetto sons ran wild in the slums; don't start none, won't be none. If ya start some, we'll empty then reload scratched off serial guns, empty another then reload again, et cetera et cetera.

We understood the law. If you let one slide, others will try to ride. Every member of the team has a lion heart and each and every one of us will bang for the pride. Our lifestyle was something we could no longer hide. We're fifteen and sixteen, getting locked up and coming home with stab wounds and bullet holes. I got locked up at fifteen, and at sixteen, I took two for the team. I was laying on a gurney, watching docs cut my scrotum to insert a flexible swab to test for lead poison before they cleaned me up to prevent gangrene.

We're getting it. At all times, fatigue pockets stood with stacks of dead presidents, us hood fellas stood flashy, diamonds on chain and bracelets were gaudy, but stood in something limo black tinted, low low, so popo didn't see the smoke from cambo and the swigs of momo, and so bystanders and foes don't see faces if we had to let off trey eights, nine mills, four fours, four fives and three eight zeros. We had money, power and respect.

Everything was right but eventually went left. We were living free till jail and death, my day-one fam is dying at an alarming rate, funerals happened yearly like un-hollydays. All we wanted to do was help our mothers put food on our plates, not stand together watching another member's soul hitchhike on a dove and flyaway. Onlookers soon after became hitchhikers. I wasn't finished mourning the first because I got bombarded with more murders. We didn't help. We hurt our mothers. I would live poor forever, if I could get back my brothers.

Urban Psalms

I spend as much time as I did on the block behind a pc, m i c, or pad to line drop. I showcase my poetic talent instead of catching two twenty cases or something more violent like heads under pillows and gats with potatoes to keep a crime scene silent. This ain't my hobby. Speaking words in spoken word keeps temptation from dragging me back to a nycha lobby. This is life to me. Blood, sweat and tears in stanzas is what you see.

Paths in life weren't chosen by me, they were made for me. They say it takes a village to raise a child. Well, I was a Juvy just doing what I saw every time I walked out my project door. I heard Roy g biv being advertised while I walked over works on the floor, possibly infected with HIV by a needle sharer scratching like they have poison ivy. I remember mommy grabbing me and sprinting to the elevator then out the lobby like a Spanish Jackie Joyner kersee, because she didn't want me to hear or see how our neighbors lived in our invisible gated community.

It didn't matter . . . I still heard and saw every time she sent me to the supermarket. I heard and saw the way of the black market, coke, dope and the blacksmiths selln blue ratchets. It was like hunts point but in the projects. Every other apartment was sitting at the table or rotating a Pyrex. I grew fond to the life of narcotics, the income, the sound of gats of power and smell of gun powder. I was a nice lil' boy going sour.

Daddy passed. Momma could no longer contain my bad ass. I was a hustler's son that admired the ways of the other bastard children that had similar fathers on the ave. They took me in like a hustln orphan to learn the life of that desperately seekn Susan, and when I learnt I became a cocaine pimp, from rice and eggs, it went to lobster and shrimp, to Moët from sugar water. I was making dollars out of fifteen cents in the slum. My profit was eighty-five percent like the blind, deaf and dumb.

I was married to the streets and so was my best men. We sported diamonds on pinkies instead of ring fingers like mafioso minority leaders, hood stars, with ghetto porn stars parlaying in five stars like young scars. The world was ours. Money machines counted the green after we broke down them rectangle bars. We lived reckless as if we had a death wish, but really, we constantly prayed to avoid death kisses from our mothers and significant others.

Slowly but surely, my homies started getting divorced. We prayed the best but expected the worst. I wore all black with the surviving soldiers circling the trap, flashers blinking as a motorcade followed a limo with a mourning mother or a weeping widow, following a hearse back-to-back. It was funerals, murals, housing tenements with a building entrance cluttered with flickering candles. All the neighborhood hustlers reminisce in plain view. Those are the days gangsters with tear drops tatted under their eye really cry.

One after another, another brother and another brother, if it wasn't jail it was murder. I knew dudes on both sides of the gun . . . some are dead or locked up forever. These are reflections of an ex-hustler, a lucky survivor of a way of life where you trade your social for a docket number or your birth for a death certificate.

Criminal Courts

Criminal court judges would threaten me, "carrasco, you better not let me see you in here one more time!" So, I went harder for the team and made sure the next charge landed me in supreme to face a different judge while pleadn innocence for any alleged crimes.

Who's that Spanish guy? That's bellaco from castle hill, he's Ill, no chill, he puts gats in mouths and force feeds iron pills. He's about his business. Don't get the poet twisted. He promotes peace, but when fulanos carry on, he explodes like protons and electrons and gun powder in shells before releasing blue top teflons.

I grew up in a time when even the hardest dude had to duck shots, when only 187 bidders tatted tear drops, when work supplies could only be bought at smoke shops, when gangsters carried metal and didn't trust glocks.

The hood raised me. I'm the offspring of guns, drugs and poverty; street corner hustlers were my guardians; my atheist parents were bosses who peeps rarely see, my idols were the ones who flaunted and lived the life of luxury.

To outsiders, I was a menace. In my blood, bordered isle I was the poster child. When I got shot, the community cheered for me; when I got locked up, they applauded; when I had my hazards blinking and high beams on taking part of a funeral motorcade, it was followed by a parade.

My Silent Entourage

When I recite, it's my heart and hurt talking, cause my mind be elsewhere. All my pieces are ghost written by the souls of the crossed over I contain within . . . I'm just the narrator. I sit in a crowd and wait for them to call my name . . . Edgar, Orlando, Ralphy, Eddie, bunca, Kris Kringle, blue, Eddie, koko, eliseo, abdul ghaffar (just to mention a few). Since my name is too long, they abbreviate it, they condense it so all I hear is introducing infinite. I walk to the mic, bow my head for a moment of silence . . . I don't tell nobody. For a few seconds, I just stay silent. The crowd thinks I'm thinking before I start spitting. They don't understand I'm quickly reminiscing before I bring the lyrical violence just as harsh as the physical violence that causes me to pause for those moments of silence. Inside, I suffer. There's pain in every word I muster; blood, sweat and invisible tears through every stanza. When I'm finished and say that's that piece, the snaps and applause go through me and reach the deceased. I never wanted to face this world alone. I feel my soldier's presence but when I'm looking in the mirror, I see my face alone . . . and it kills me. Them not being present isn't pleasant. When I tap keys, push a pencil or pen . . . I'm instantly reunited with my kin. My poetry is basically about an era starting from nineteen eighty-four to the present cause the epidemic isn't over. Time, the liar and the reaper, teamed up and took many men; on the streets, we roamed; from streets, we claimed but never really owned. Like I said, I write with hurt and my heart because my mind is elsewhere. I'm constantly thinking of a contraption to keep me writing while I'm sleeping, so I can see their faces while I'm dreaming.

In the Beginning

When the game first started for us, the ole g's tried to stop us from making money. They pulled out blickys, took our rock, told us to take off sneakers and socks and not to move till they got up the block. Us youngens stood there frozen . . . it was okay, we weren't scared. We didn't own gats like they bared. All we knew is that we got next and live by castle hill's slogan . . . Never ran, never will. Mofos, we ain't run'n. We're in the big park by the sandbox bumping what will soon be trademarked tops. We didn't have to jet from narcs cause they didn't know the trap was open. Our only problem was them ole g's front'n.

They came and came again. Only if they knew each time was getting more and more dangerous for them. In-between stick ups, we saved up for protection. Instead of splitting PC, we put all that money back in. I'm a hustler's son, put out the word that I needed to go metal shopping, the blacksmith came to the bricks loaded and left with a bunch of 1s, 5s and 10s . . . aight let them haters come back again. Now, we're a bunch of brave-hearted ados with a crack flow but armed with revolvers semis and fully autos.

Here they come . . . to them, it's a quick come up of a few g's, click clack. Before they reached, everybody pulls out gats and puts them bitches on their knees. My codees are dying to squeeze. They want to make examples outta these cats that been sticking us up since the days when we were trying to build clientele by giving out samples . . . that would've made the trap hot. So, instead of merkn them, I did what they did to us. I made 'em take off their sneakers and socks, gun butted them and make them run barefoot down the block. They never came back. We became too strong.

Bellaco ... the name rang thru the slums like the bell on that lil' white cart pushed by the neighborhood viejo, sell'n coquito, rip to orlandito. He went back-to-back with "albertito". When things had to fly, I could definitely count on him to let things go. Without him, it would've taken longer to reach a kilo. Before he was taken from me, we reached that reign supreme level. I just continued the dienasty with the army, battling the four Devils; not just lust, envy, hate and jealousy, but beelzebub, satan, lucifer and the reaper.

I was nice cutting Coke cookies with a gem star. I carved hard grams like Edward scissor hands. I had to be in order to keep up with the demand. Fives went to the left, to the right went tens. All night, I was separating stones, then filling up Tupperware in drug dens with my men to mend broken homes. We had big plans and they were being executed just as expected. Organization was tight, peeps had no choice but to respect it. We went from freelancers to block runners to legends of the present time.

We got tired of dealing with the season's elements, sun, snow, rain and wind while stacking dead presidents; so, we moved from outdoors to lobbies in housing tenements. The move didn't stop the flow but it did stop observation sales. Caspers were sent in to no prevail. If we didn't know you, you couldn't cop; if a fiend says they knew you, they got dropped, cosigning strangers could get us all knocked. The trap was impenetrable, we had it Fort Knox locked.

Stab wounds, head, torso and back shots ... pause ... puss and blood forced its way out gauze; felony mug shots, dockets, population, incarceration. My day ones are succumbing to knives and guns in street wars. Dudes that got put on got life, got high on their supply or died. There's only a handful still by my side. Bellaco . . . boss status, legends, Bronx capos.

In My Genes

I'm the type of dude that would be an asset to any team. I'm a hustler's son, the game is in my genes. I have a lot to bring to the table. Since I was a kid, I was doing a street bid. I watched everything pops did. He would pull up on the ave in his Plymouth wagon with the wood panel'n, jump out, bump hash and reefa, get back in and drive off count'n math. I learnt to never speak unless spoken to and never volunteer information rules as a youngen. I remembered faces of custys and places of transactions. I remember him never leavn the crib without guns, clips and extra ammunition. When dad died, I revisited those people and places, not as a passenger but as a hustler.

I knew the ropes. It was just a different era. Instead of hash and weed, it was Coke fiends were after. Not the norm, it was Coke in a form other than just powder . . . crack . . . the new drug for the party user. Since everybody knew me, it was easy for bosses to give me opportunity. They did, they gave me plenty. I didn't even need money. All they said was see them when I was empty. They got theirs, I got mine. Everybody was happy.

I grew up in a project building where most of the children were boys. I mean, there was a lot of us. We all had one thing in common, and that was poverty. The bond we had was incredible. We were inseparable. Gettn paper together was inevitable. We did. Instead of poor kids, now were Bellaco. Since then, I never strayed. Everything I did, I did with them, for them and vice versa. There were no outsiders. I ate, they ate; they ate, I ate. We kept each other up.

Like a boulder in the concrete jungle, I stood stationary when teammates got locked up. No matter how much time was served, they'll know where to find me; when they had to go on the run, they knew ill lead the race; when they all died one by one, I sat by headstones and spent time with each and every one of them. I read birth and death dates, then sat motionless, remembering what took place to have marble rock sticking out grass with my friend's face.

Although I'm loved by many, I never sought for cover or switched teams when the weight on my back got heavy. The way I rolled with one hundred dudes is the way I'll roll alone, if ninety-nine of them got sent home . . . and I proved it when all my guys heard the fat lady's music, I was Dolo, holding down the trap. It's all I knew and wasn't prepared to let it go. I was an army of one till the come up of the new generation . . . I'm the type of dude that would be an asset to any team. I'm a hustler's son, the game is in my genes.

Puerto Rican Sosa

Here I am, the puerto rican Sosa. I'll leave the backs of your fake ass scars all over. Guns spark like in sparks steak house, heads of crime families get taken out, columbian neck ties like my cousins do, tongues stickn out of where Adam apples protrude. I'm no street brawler. I'll 44 ya, then boil ya. Bellaco, the motto's la costra nostra.

I ran through millions. My fingertips are rich. I was married to the game. I divorced the white girl. The streets still pay me alimony. Ain't that a bitch? I parlay at spots like a star, two shooters with me, two in the front waiting on that signal in the car. I don't sleep. Sleep's the cousin of death. So, if ya creep up on me buyaka, rock-a-bye baby sayonara.

If we do what it does and I don't finish you, but I know I hit you, it's a trip to the local hospital walk into emergency, mask gloves desert e, and get it on with your crew in the visiting room. I'll leave one alive till he tells me your room number, then it's triangle at temple. It's murder.

I keep hollows for dumb dumbs. I keep brass tips to riddle whips. Either way, they spray from extended's, vroom vroom choppers like chips. When they stay cocked back, I reverse them clips, re-chamber, then back to dismember. Bellaco is neutral . . . just so affiliated, when it's time to pop my nikkas, is color coordinated.

When it comes to drama, I'm the prez like Obama. I sit back and watch video stream of my pañas removing threats like Osama. Before we throw you in the water, we take a snap shot to send to your mother so she could know starting today she could mourn ya. Her son is no longer.

Pusher

I'm yo pusher, I got what you want. Here, take this consignment, when come for mine and you don't have my money ready . . . it's murder. I'm violent. I ain't your friend. This here is work and we're business men. Don't play me. I'll home invade merk wives and abort newborn babies. There's no excuses for shorts. I don't wanna hear shit; fuck, you pay me. I got shooters on da payroll eager to earn their wages. Ayo, they said four days and it's the fifth day . . . somebody's gonna lay for that delay. All I care is about myself, everybody else is expendable for wealth. If cribs get raided, it's your loss; if you go to jail, call your mother or baby's momma for bail. I ain't your boss. Oh, you got drama, handle yours. I'll be in Havana blazn cubanas and come back after the wars. If ya die . . . oh well, I'll give your right-hand man a try. If he fucks up, y'all will be bffs in the sky. This life stole my sorrow emotion; since both of them are has beens, I'll feed their competition to keep my paper coming in. Genocide . . . I take a part in it. Bloodshed painted the hood red. So, I made an art out of it. Cross me, and you'll be the newest exhibit in the projects, a picture of pain, an abstract portrait of the game . . . the name will be "another statistic of cocaine".

Di-me- lo, I heard ya need yayo. Okay, okay, I got ya but if you don't pay, it's another corpse sprinkled with perico like I do. Shit . . . my hit men get paid off I o u's, they're like debt collectors that make sure they collect before leavn ya like head vegans in I c u. I'm yo pusher.

0-100

I went from 0 to 100 real quick. I kept myself on idle by blowing out smoke real thick. Life had me angry; so, I was a silent time bomb . . . like a rolex you didn't hear a tick, cause the lie kept me calm.

I wasn't a menace to society; society was menacing me. Look at him, he's a thug, he's a hustler. They didn't overstand that I was a little boy when I lost my father . . . the breadwinner. So, I had hatred for poverty. Without him, when I looked into the cabinets for food, I heard my breathing echo from shelves being empty.

Our stomachs ached waiting for government cheese, milk, bread, kix and kaboom, that's why as soon as I got with the white girl, I jumped the broom.

Mama knew she wasn't legal; so, she never considered herself an in-law. She told me she's no good, but I wanted to get out the hood regardless if she was making me an outlaw. My eyes are green, but they stood red and my fingers stood numb from touching her . . . she was pure. After every L, life was an easier hell; after every flip, I was getting closer to picking up where dad fell.

THC contained the beast within me. I knew without it I would've been catching A1 felonies; cause on my dark road to riches, I sensed snakes and saw phonies that should've been dressed their best laid-back listening to their eulogies.

I probably would've been a lifer without face-time or ciphers. I had to speak to myself . . . inf, he deserves it but he's not worth the time handed out for a murder; it'll take some convincing, but I'll give in and smile like . . . "you, lucky motherfucker". I have to stay in the streets to do the struggling for my widowed mother.

The dutch stood between my lips as I moved the pyrex in a motion like females with hoola hoops on their hips. I couldn't touch it or it'll be raw contaminated; so, I left it there like ole timers conversing with a square. I was getting high selling get high to get by. I didn't like my reality; so, I lived a lie.

Why Now?

Why now? Why after all these years? . . . I spoke to a mutual friend of myself and the person I speak of. He tells me something that blew my mind, he said did you hear about so and so . . . Just hearing her name along with that phrase fucked me up because nothing sweet usually comes after. Inf, she looks so different. You won't believe that it's her. What's wrong with her I ask . . . He says, she's sniffing boy lines. I asked him how did he know and he says she's with a tecato, he turned her on, now she's running around the hood asking for credit. As a matter of fact, she just got beat up for owing dough. When I find her, it's not going to be pretty. I know her mother and son personally, so, whatever actions I take, they'll back me completely. That doogie hurt friends and family, so, I'll handcuff her to a steam pipe or something else stationary and watch her go through three days of agony, she can scream and fuss, yell and cry but I'll have no pity for the invisible monkey. The last time I was in this situation, I let them free, I felt bad for my cuffed homie . . . After that day, it took a few months to find him in one of the many local shooting galleries . . . By that time, he was already telling me that there was nothing I could do and that he was sorry. I don't want her to get in that deep, to the point where who she was goes through eviction and all you see is just a body of addiction. Heroin isn't something people can fight alone, because when they're alone is when temptation roams and their will power gets overthrown. It's amazing to me how people already know the effects of that drug and still take that first hit, knowing how hard it is to quit. She held a good job; she was probably ready to retire. What hurts is that she was raised right and is pretty but now I know she's somewhere seeing how life can be ugly. Some dirty dudes are offering her head nod for head bob, she's probably on a strip selling a brick for a bag . . . I hope she doesn't have it that bad, she's probably chippn in five with dan the dope man and somewhere random itching and scratching sick cause dan ran with the dope in his hand. Like I said in the beginning, her beauty and upbringing aren't going to stop hustlers from getting their money, her pretty face will be all bloody with a bruised body. I have to start circling traps and bring her back before she feels the effect kicks in slower sniffn and turns to leavn tracks. I can picture her family shedding tears . . . At forty-four, why now? Why after all these years?

Trap Life Narration

My pointer and thumb went numb from pinchn gems and slabbn crumbs for many moons and suns, my skin has burned holes . . . The result of guns. My heart is scared beyond repair, it has groups of four keloid bubbles vertically and one horizontally as a tally for those no longer breathn air. There's rage in my pen and anger in my spoken verses when I write or spit to paint pictures of crimeys that no longer worry 'bout when the first is, for rushes, cause they're lying in the back of hearses.

Who am I? The hardest griot in NY, you'll overstand why when you hear my rhyming narration on the life of pitchn bassn sniffn injections incarceration and slug penetration.

Inf is A-grade like top-notch material, you could put soda on my stanzas to make hard or fine-grind them to make bundles of lethal, got that speed ball flow, I'll make ya lean and move slow then make ya spaz like snortn lines of pure blow.

The streets know me, I was the first one thought of when cats had fantasies of moving puree or her-ron like I'm trappers Ricardo Montalban . . . The fast life . . . I had the pedal to the metal speeding through death streets and murder avenues like the autobahn. Anything non-monetary was secondary, keep that bullshit to yourself and carry on, I'm carrying bombs and arms watchn for movements and climate change in my environment.

I couldn't stay still, walked from Randall to Castle Hill to Seward to Olmstead back to Randall like an undercover ghost buster, ya know dem narcs with the day's color tryn to creep and put slime on ya. There's a science to violence . . . criminology . . . I studied it to learn theories, on the road to the riches it made me a better me, I should've made it a hustler study group to avoid the head bows, clasped hands and all the RIPs.

One More Time to See Them

It'll be a red-carpet event. I would gather friends and family. My phone, iPad and digital recorder will be capturing life-long memories, all of their favorite foods and beverages will be over burners and behind bars ready, because they are so loved. I'll even let in paparazzi to have a photo frenzy. Everybody will get the opportunity to take selfies, it'll be the celebration of a lifetime. They'll be tears of joy, they'll be massive smiles and laughter, everyone will be holding onto and hugging each other . . . a beautiful extravaganza. "Oh, wow, look at him", "Oh, wow, look at her", "hey, so and so, do you remember me?", "I love you", "long time no see", "I knew you'll grow to be very handsome / pretty", "you have no clue how much you mean to me". That's what I'll hear walking around the party. Me, I'll let everyone get the love out their system, since I'm the host I'll get the last hour with them. I'll study and mentally record every nook and cranny, every mole and freckle, facial expressions, mannerisms and voice tones, so I could close my eyes and see and hear them again when the gathering is over and they go back home to the father.

Ready for the World

I didn't know if the world was ready me. Oh well, it's too late to prepare, ears can't close. So, there's no choice but to listen to the lemniscate as I street life elaborate, spoken word orchestrate, I grab M I C's and mc till third eyes dilate. Infinite is the Obama of Urbana; I pop fiction swiftly and deadly like the seals that went on the mission to merk Osama. My forte is ye, scrilla, jail and murder. So, I write about cocaine, money, and prison time for gunshot trauma because of street corner drama to control the flow of the almighty dollar, when slugs fly its boom bye bye for two hustlers, one gets life the others a goner. I'm a drug dealer. I deal with drugs . . . I scribe crack and give it away for free to create addiction, if you read me once it's a guarantee that you'll relapse again, I need the entire world to start abusing me, my hipspoketry. Life to me was fucked up, my dudes got sent back and sent up, state and fed up, I hate when children cry for daddy or mommy at the end of a V I, just like I hate the smell of embalming fluid and wake makeup when someone dies. So, I made it business to go back to the hood and reach my hand into hell on earth's fire and pull out pushers, and all other type of hustlers before they fry. The ghetto listens to me because I was them growing up in poverty. Instead of glamorizing the game, I showcase my hurt and pain from those ill-gotten gains, the hustle wasn't fun to me, come with me to my local cemetery, so we could visit spots that hold loved ones' remains, then look at me to see if I'm frowning or smiling . . . I wasn't happy at all, but after the first died I said I'm going all out . . . for him I'll ball, I would rise and fall, then another would die, I said the same thing . . . for him I'll ball, I would rise and fall . . . I said that over and over again, we'll be in that cemetery for an hour saluting all my friends. There was nobody to ball for anymore, I'm trying to explain that to all y'all caught up in the arena of C and D continuing to want more.

Fit In

I want to fit in so bad that I'm willing not to be myself just to be noticed. Playing sports, reading magazines to keep up with the style and trend are my favorite things to do amongst other stuff but when I see them, they're are not into sports. So, I act like I'm not as well. Their statement of fashion is sagging. I do that when I'm around them cause it makes me look ruff. I don't like the way I feel high but when they pass the L, I feel it'll be disrespectful if I didn't puff puff then pass to the next individual. All it does is make me hungry and lazy . . . this isn't for me, but to be a part of them . . . I'll make it be.

Time passes. I no longer choke on the passes. In fact, sometimes I take four of five chokes before I pass . . . I got used to it at last. Now I'm going to weed spots to cop the loud, I'm spending all my saved allowance. Instead of buying jerseys and uniforms and so on . . . I'm getting my smoke on. I'm part of the fam. What's up fellas? What are we doing tonight? We 're going to club! Yesssss, I've never been to a club. What time are we meeting up? When night falls, so we can travel in the dark to cop an eight ball . . . cool, I like pool . . . The homies start laughing. Hahahaha, stop playing, fool. I left it at that. It must mean something else.

Night falls. We meet at the train to ride to Manhattan. Yo fellas, where y'all going? That's the uptown side. Just come on. We're going to make a pit stop to pick up that eight ball . . . the train came . . . we went inside. A few stops later we got off, one of the guys says stay here I'll go get it. I say, na. I'm going to come with you. We go. Everyone else stays. We walk a block, go up to the third floor and my friend knocks on a door, it opens. What you want? My friend says an eight ball, the door closes then opens again, they exchange, it's all new to me . . . kind of strange. We head back to the train and meet back up with the fellas.

Sup y'all got that? My friends say yup, now we're back on the train but going downtown . . . Ding dong doors shut. A few stops later, we arrive in midtown, its 'bout to go down! We walk to the club but have to wait until the bouncers let us in all at same time . . . they let us in. We're mingling with the ladies. A few minutes later, my boy says, get the fellas and meet me in the bathroom. I'm thinking, it's get high time, it was but this time it wasn't weed, it was some powdery stuff in white lines . . . one by one, they all take this little straw and sniff it. I did it . . . Why did I do it! I feel amped up and I'm sweating standing still, my boys are on the dance floor acting ill, it made me feel ill, but then again, after a while I was copping my own eight balls of coke at will.

We started putting coke in weed and made coolies, when there was no coke, we decided that crack and weed would give us a similar high as coolies but people called them woolies. Now I love getting high and binging, I started getting stingy, my boys started getting mad because I wasn't sharing, the ones I wanted to be so much around and the ones that said they had love for me are no longer caring. Forget them. I was the one with the money. The one day I thought to myself . . . how did I get myself into this position? I'm back to being alone but with all sorts of addictions.

Poverty's Home

If you go visit poverty, you'll see mr. and mrs. welfare
    walking the streets,
future dead/felon kids hanging on the chains that remain
    where swings once swung,
Piss and the stench of crack in buildings are
    welcoming mats,
Fiends are doormen,
    addicts are the concierge,
The pusher runs the elevator as hell's waiter.
Grandma moms and daughter sit on chairs
    with distressful stares,
Grandpa and dad still got their fatigues on,
    thinking they're in ww2 or 'nam,
Televisions constantly play the same show . . . Snow,
Spanish men wear fist picks in fros, black brothers wear
    guallaveras and chancletas it's a diverse but poor area,
People here weep oceans of sorrow knowing yesterday was
    just as today was,
Knowing tomorrow will have the same woes of today,
    the salt in our diet gets wiped away.
Fire escapes and terraces are where imaginary vacations
    take place,
Old man sam owns the vehicle used as the local
    school zone van,
People ask the bodega owners for credit, standing next to
    signs saying "no credit",
Funeral homes advertise deals,
Hearse drivers drive around the hood to figure
    the fastest route to the cemetery,
Liquor stores took food stamps, now ebt,
That's life you see in poverty in just one block.
Now if you visit a house where poverty lives,
You'll see hungry kids constantly opening

empty refrigerators,
Cracked tiles lead a path to two bedrooms and one bathroom,
The three or four people in each bedroom shout out "next"
    when they gotta use the bathroom,
Mattresses on floors are beds, sofas, recliners
    and dinner tables,
Mom's and dad's old twelve-inch tracks in crates are chairs,
Telephone cords had no phone attached, so we used it to
    air-dry hand-washed clothes,
Heat came from boiling water on stoves and in ovens,
Air conditioning meant every window, top and bottom
    was open,
Mildew and mold painted Monas on halls,
Smashed roach remains remain on walls,
Buckets are used to catch water, leaking from pipes
    leading to faucets,
At times, they were also used to flush toilets.

Acapella

When I spit acapella, it's education to youngsters and opera to gangsters and hustlers. Infinite is a tenor, the poverotti of drugs, guns and death in poor societies, experience made me, in the year 1971 mom dukes gave birth to a child of urban apostrophe, in the year 1984 I became a crack baby, na . . . moms wasn't smoking, that's a metaphor meaning I was a young pimp getting money by pushing that white whore, off-white and beige raw, poverty had me enlist in street tours, life or death drug wars, project apartments became Pyrex labs for girl chemists, when they kicked in doors we couldn't say we was studying science, the two twenty charges say we brewed violence and was a part of the pestilence, it's just when it came to eviction notices and starvation the poor formed a resistance to help ourselves instead of dying slowly on government assistance. I'm not trying to be the hardest, I'm going to get mine, but I'm not claiming to be the largest, I'm in a lane of my own, not following and can't be followed by other artists, my style of rhyme is like my fingerprint, without introduction whatever I touch the people will know it's mine . . . The flow is intricate, narcotic, I'm hooked on phonics and Ebonics my third eye is bionic.

My grammar got hit by rays of gamma, so my vocabulary is brolic, when it comes to blood cash, I hulk smash but what I write and recite isn't cloud captions like the comics, I really lived it that's why I paint pictures so vivid and graphic. Surviving the death wave like a phlebotomy surfer made me a murder ink image writer, an urban photographer, a trap life bar blower.

More Losses Than Gains

Writing to save lives saved my life. It's going to be a decade since I wrote my first piece, if I didn't, I probably would've still been on the block filthy, gat cocked, a few bs or packs gettn blood money, locked up or when thought of, the memory would've ended with RIP. The urge to create kept me in the lab instead of in the kitchen chefn then breakn chips of cookies to pack in slabs. At this point, I was writing for myself; it was a release of bloodshed visuals and tears that wouldn't cry.

I found a way to get off the block, now I needed income other than pushn trees, lean, soft or rock, the game was all I knew because when I first started, I blew, I was going to hustle till I went to God, at no point in my life I would think to myself . . . Damn, I need a job. All I had to do was cop a few grams to make a few grand, whole things to pop bands, two colors and a name was my unbeatable brands, I didn't have to advertise, the material spoke for itself. All clientele was mine, I'm the fuckn man.

Brainstorming how to legally cake for a prolonged period of time had me diggn in the crate, I'm used to living a certain lifestyle, I was spending when I shouldn't, whatever came to mind I copped it, wasn't going to settle for balling on a budget. That's exactly what it became, when it came to splurging, I had to refrain . . . I would tell myself . . . Inf, fall back, it's been about three years since reed-up with her-on or Caine.

That hunger that I had when I was living in poverty came back to the OG, that hunger that made me a better me, that hunger that made my day ones RIP, it's time, time to get this shmoney. The ones that got lucky to stay alive, I got you, my new hustle arrived, poetry . . . urban-derived, they say the game is to be sold not told. So, I'm pitchn bloody currency since I'm one of the first to witness the sport unfold.

Cream on top of cream, I was just a teen living the so-called American Dream, so was the team. Before digitals, we had tricks for beams, had that good good for all fiends, gold diamonds, something foreign pur'n, how much Vicky's? . . . Na, I'm not sayn not'n, timbs, wife B, jeans with pockets swollen, violate, we'll turn African and blow guns, we did it we did it, we're rich . . . I wish, my running mates got life or rest in a ditch, birth date, death date ain't that a bitch?

It was supposed to last forever, besides my homie beck, everyone that died was a statistic of murder, I go to my homies' crib to look at pics of them when they were alongside their mother, sons and daughters. To make sure they don't die in vain, I paint pictures of pain, every word is a still frame, for not using hunger wisely I've lost more than I could ever gain.

Time Paid Ransom

I lived every day as if tomorrow. I would be a lifer or statistic of murder, I showed massive love to friends and fam and let slugs fly in walk-bys, ride-bys, drive-bys to let enemies know where we stand, kept the liquor on low levels running the streets but blazed sticky choc, beef and broc till it looked like I was making moves asleep on and off the block.

I'm not a big drinker, I'm a deep thinker like my thoughts derive from the equator, after every vanilla with earth they get deeper, I face time while thinking of those that crossed over then I feel like using mental telepathy to converse with all the fellas six feet under, I see caskets skeletons earth worms and maggots when I'm about to body an urban stanza by pushing a pen over paper.

So many of my men died. I wonder, while they're in the heavens, do they think that me and the few that survived are Angels because the afterlife is norm to them. From the outside in, it'll look like the reaper was the keeper of my kin because of the high rate of death while trying to bread-win in the belly amongst beast of jinn. The root of evil brought seeds closer to the devil. Whoever wrote in God we trust on paper were connivers, many men worshipped currency till they became cadavers punctured by daggers and slugs that made 'em stagger.

I staggered and fell, got back up, recouped, re'd up and when back to the streets of death and avenues of hell to make blasphemous sells in the parish of the perished. I was doing the same thing as murder victims in the slums not caring for the outcome, my only care was income, I was trap napped. Time paid my ransom.

Writing

I go into a trance-like state when I'm writing, deep thought before there's lead traces or ink starts seeping. I become that person place or thing at that point of time in my mind while I'm scribing. My surroundings at that moment are irrelevant. The only thing I see is poetry, if I'm going to write about slavery, I become a slave . . . Crack crack, that's the sound of the whip as it scars backs.

I'm tied to a tree along with many other men in captivity hearing the moans of our women being raped on plantations in front of our children. Thump thump thump, that's my wife's, my child's and my bleeding, bare-feet running, sweating, searching for freedom through fields of cotton, gravel roads and woods trying to stay ahead of trotting hoofs because if they catch up it'll be a snug noose.

They call that concrete imagery; I look at it as if a soul from a son of a tribe is speaking through me. At times, I write and you might not know what I'm writing about until the end. They drugged her before the knife passed creating an eight-inch gash. Blood-drenched rags were all over, her man is there too but there's nothing he can do as they cut away but say . . . it's going to be okay. He's holding her hand watching what's unfolding, what he's seeing he's not believing but it's actually happening.

It could kill her if he tries to stop them. So, he just stands there and witnesses his baby being born through Caesarian. When I scribe about my past and the loss of many men, I get into the deepest part of my thought process, my mind roams in another realm, it's like being awake but going through R.E.M.

While I try to get to a level where I actually can converse with them, I'll take you to a point where we screamed out, "yeah, we made it" to a point where I'm in standing next to one of their caskets and everything in-between as we chased that street dream. Every day, I just think, and write poetry. It's a process to my sanity.

A Justifiable Suicide

They say if you commit suicide, you won't go to heaven. So, I should blow out my brains and go to hell to cause mayhem . . . the devil prays to God to make sure he stops that temptation, he doesn't want to deal me, I'll torture him for all the souls he stole. His lies won't work, his fire won't burn, he'll be powerless in his kingdom, I see three sixty plus my epidermis is soaked with wisdom. I'll search the darkness for my homies, so I can point them to the sun and free them from the evil son. Since I'm under, I'll divide and conquer. Hey, goon and goblin, if you help me, I'll give you power to see clearer, I'll douse your flame so you can feel flesh like before death, you'll no longer have to live all day as if it was night when I point you to the light, before I point . . . what you have to do is, do for someone else as I did for you, help them see clear and douse their flame. Eventually, the devil will be by himself. I was stuck on a rock and a hard place; he's stuck under the rock, trapped and lonely in a hot place. It'll be just me and him in an eternal clash of fire vs water.

A Living Legend

I'm so fly when I walk, I get jet lag, retired 15 years ago and dudes still haven't reached my amount of pushed slabs. Inf's a veteran of raw, after a twenty-year tour, I became a ghetto seal that mastered the art of war, I can go all out and slaughter or divide and conquer, that decision depends on what position I'm in . . . If ya come at me or my kin, I'm going huntn. If ya frontn, I'll infiltrate and begin separation.

In eighty-four, I was twelve but considered a crack baby because it was the year of cooked Coke, the streets didn't have a titty for me to suck on, so I got my boil on to pass bombs. Mix'n that badder was a generic form of similac powder, I just didn't digest it, I cooked kit, dried it, chopped it, advertised it, and bumped it for profit . . . that's how I maintained a more than 2000 calorie daily diet.

I got fat, I mean from a few grams, I gained weight, I'm dropping off and picking up across the tri-state, that white girl had me beating my chest like King Kong as if these bx streets was the Empire State, they tried to shoot me down but I kept a grip, recouped and vowed to always keep a full clip, if they came at me again and tried to stop my relations with Ms. Blanca, they're going to meet the father, that shouldn't be blasphemy because I'll be doing a soul living in hell a favor.

From a kid with peach fuzz, I went to a teen with fades, fatigues, timbs and dark shades to an adult with a receding hairline . . . that was an eighty-four to two thousand timelines of white crime, went from a boy to a man pushn ace deuces treys nicks and dimes. Since then, I've been manufacturing on white lines, I don't need a connection anymore. All I have to do is write Cee aRe Aye Cee Kay on a Pyrex to produce crack like back in the day. My lyrics are pure ye, fish-scale wordplay.

My style is unorthodox like when a lefty and a righty box. If any bird takes shots, I'll riddle them with holes . . . deadly chicken pox, there's a viral disease, everybody is screaming out thug life . . . small pacs, keep ya eyes open and stop breathing when squeezing . . . I paid attention in hard knocks, 10 to every?? . . . Na, I can't pass off the recipe for hard rocks, cause nobody will ever do it like bellaco on these blown-up spots.

Code of the Streets, Part 1

It was a regular day before that knock . . . Who is it? No one's expected so I instantly insert the magazine in my rubber grip. Inf, hurry it's me . . . I know the voices of my team, I open the door, all bloody my homie just drops on the floor. I pull my kin in, shut the door and start searching for his wounds, where ya hit at, homie! No response. His shirt is all red, he's passed out, he has a pulse so I know he's not dead. He needs immediate help but I don't know the circumstances that led to this point, if he went out and put work in and the cops are searching, going to the local er's will definitely send him to the joint, or if a death squad is lurking, they'll know the same . . . Finish him in the o.r. It's a part of the game. If I keep him here, he'll die quickly, his breathn is getting heavy. I had to react fast. Stay with me, mo, I lift up his shirt and see three holes, I turn him around and see three holes, he'll make it if the slugs didn't hit major arteries or organs, I picked him up, rushed to the garage and put him in the back of the Benz wagon, pulled out and pulled his blood-soaked range in, got back in the Benz, put the pedal to the metal on the express way the way I would in a get-a-way to reach a quiet neighborhood with a desolate area near a hospital on the outskirts of New York. I pulled over, checked his pulse again, he's alive. I took him out the whip and laid him gently on the sidewalk, got back in, pulled out my rubber grip and licked . . . pow, pow, pow, pow, I parked down the block and called 911 . . . Hello, what's your emergency? I just heard shots, I tell them where, hang up and stay till I see help arrive, helpless. All I could do is pray he stays alive. I changed the crime scene just in case it's needed for an alibi, real dudes do real things, if he dies while I stand guard calling family and friends outside, I'll never know why.

To be continued . . .

Code of the Streets, Part 2

I follow the ambulance to the hospital. One by one my team pulls up, strapped up ready for war.

Inf, what happened? I can't tell you, only he knows. He drove to my crib hit up, then passed out before I can get the who, what, where and why. Send wifey in, split the fellas up and watch the entrances and exits, you . . . you watch the room, if it's not a doctor or nurse . . . no one gets next to him! I have to get to my crib and burn his whip, they'll be looking for it, if it was an unfinished hit.

Call me as soon as you find out something. I'll be back. I get home and inspect the car, there's no bullet holes in the doors or seats that means he got hit at home or in the street. I change my bloody clothes and put them in a bag, I grab a container of gas and a sheet to cover the blood-soaked front seat, I get in and drive to a dirt road and begin the arson, I stood there till it was just a metal skeleton. When the fire stopped and was just smoking, I turned around and started walking back to my house to get my car. So many things are going through my head, whoever touched my right hand made man is dead, along with their set or crime family! It's on, now somebody has to deal with me, I need to find out what happened immediately so I can begin the reaction to their actions. I get home, take a shower to wash of the attempted murder, put on my vest and fatigues, grab my machine gun, pour a glass of henny and sit waiting for the call on my recliner, blazing a godfather. My phone rings, what's up, talk to me! . . . Inf, he was up and talking, we know everything! The doctors tried, Inf but he . . . he died. Get everybody out the hospital and bring wifey to me!

To be continued . . .

Code of the Streets, Part 3

As I'm pacing back and forth looking through the window for headlights, I'm destroying everything in sight. My cup shattered on the wall, henn is all over the floor, I've never been this angry before. I'm used to death but not so close to home. There goes the motorcade of lights. I open up eagerly anticipation info. The head of my street team and wifey approach and enter. Infinite, he's gone! They killed my baby! . . . I'm so sorry . . . they'll pay! You're going to stay here; your house is no longer safe. Homie, talk to me. Who did it? He told me to tell you it was the blue jag. Okay, okay, Hun, stay here. I pass her a gun; homie lets go, there's work that needs to be done. Na Inf, stay here, we got it, tell us who's the target, I'll roll with merk and homi . . . na, this time it's on me! We leave security with wifey and head out to search for the foes in the city. Inf, who drives the blue jag? The blue jag isn't a car, it's a stamp from across town, who owns it? He'd been pushing cowards off blocks by sending these sorts of messages. The message was received clearly, the response he gets is going to be just as clear, I keep my enemies close, I know where he lives and we're near. I knew he'll be here, that's the head of blue jag with the blue durag. Okay, he's finished . . . damn right, I'm gonna bust this left, pull over and we jump out and run up on him . . . Let's do it. Ayo blue . . . this is for . . . Blue jag got a full mag. The head got cut. The body collapsed. Now, my right hand can rest in peace.

The End

Split Personality

He's the type of dude that'll force violators to play Russian roulette with automatic weapons, torture is his specialty so when offered . . . most take the roulette option. He's pure evil, I knew him well. All I can do was watch as he kills . . . I'm a spectator of death whenever he's around.

I couldn't have stopped him even if I tried because he was overpowering, his strength was overwhelming, I used to pray . . . please don't cross his path because it'll be your home going. I couldn't tell anybody because they would've thought I was crazy and I couldn't call the authorities because they would've arrested me, so I let it be.

People feared me because they feared him, since we were together all the time, they figure I conspired with the murderer. You know how many bodies I fought at trial because of him. All the liars keep circling the lineup pictures and pointing their fingers saying that they're one hundred percent sure that I'm the one they saw committing the ultimate crime. My lawyer thought me ruthless, when that's far from what the truth is.

The money for my defense wasn't mine, it's all from his crimes, if I didn't use it, I would've faced the music . . . Ya know, a chorus from a jury and a verse from the judge before hearing guilty. Family and friends distanced themselves, they figured it's not always just a coincidence that whenever he kills, I'm there and that the reason I beat cases are because of technicalities . . .

They won't understand me. I'm tired of watching death and being held accountable for his crimes. One day, I gained courage and faced him. Today's the last time I witness your madness! Your last kill was your final homicide! I pulled my gun . . . and committed suicide.

I Had a Dream

I had a dream that I died, what's scary is that I was happy. In fact, I was ecstatic, when it was coming to an end, I was trying to fall back into a deep sleep till I heard the third alarm beep, death was a beautiful thing.

I didn't see how I passed; however, I saw the realm of forever, that overshadowed the trauma drama. Amazement is an understatement; I was overwhelmed in the moment. The sun rained rays, night was just as bright as daylight, time didn't exist there.

That saltwater process was trying to occur, tears of joy . . . but I held them back because I didn't want my vision to get blurred. My sight was set on things so surreal that was the only time I would share my shoes so others can feel what I feel.

Deceased family and friends were all alive, my dad opened his arms and yelled . . . come here, son . . . I'm in awe of being in the arms of my father ten years his senior, he's as healthy as can be . . . no cancer.

The best friends I ever had were no longer in white zipper bags, I'm giving them all hugs, they're like Inf, that's enough, I'm like na, my brothers, without y'all life was tuff, but I did all I had to do to shine like a diamond in the rough.

There're no knife wounds in torsos, heads no longer have bullet holes, there's no tubes, stitches, staples, gauze, bandages, no glue sealing lips and eye lids, no bad, just lovely eternal bids. I had a dream that I died, what's scary is that I was happy.

Titanium Bars

My bars are hard like titanium, others are soft like lines in aluminum, realness is something we don't have in common, I'm da truth, these frauds are carbon, sloppy copies of my cronies, capo title plagiarism, that nonsense don't sit right with my dogs, I'd be like sante they'd be like na Inf, let us sic 'em, na it's okay for them to use their imagination to spit fiction, I rather them do that than try to make a trap and get found somewhere in critical condition. I know some that got an ill flow and spit crack but never touched blow, I can spit a slalom of what makes skiers frozen like a cocaine olympian, if I gathered it all from start to end I'll have a snow mountain with faces of dead men like Rushmore, there won't be just four, many dropped, if I put 'em all, the mountain will look like faces of hip hop, we saw a lucrative rush and wanted more in God we trust, gunpowder ignited turning flesh and bone to ash and dust, we was in love with the white girl and had a richness lust. No homo, but I kissed my homies the first, second and third day at wakes and before we let doves go, I broke nights splurging on go-aways, cause the next day dudes had to turn in on sentencing day, that's that shit dudes can't speak in depth 'bout with made up spit, I can go deeper like police, yellow tape, lights, crowds a body and a mother screaming bloody murder cause her child's blood is all over . . . I heard that high pitch yell over and over like hurt Mariah's and I will never get rid of those mental visions, not even with the best kush and sour so I put 'em on paper to paint pictures of death without actually drawing a bloody scythe and the reaper.

There's a Reason

There's a reason why I did why I did. A reason why I went through so much as a kid.
There's a reason why I did everything as every other kid, but they're dead, I lived.
I did nothing really different.
We sold drugs, carried guns, the moment we stepped out the door, we risked our life and our freedom.
They lost their lives, I'm physically free.
My mind is also free, just with so much hurtful memories of the things I've seen.
I'm forever scarred.
There're a lot reasons why.
Most of my friends were older. I go to where they rest forever.
Now I'm like twenty years their senior.
That's the same reason why I'm six years older than my father.
I saw many cry, so many asked me why?
I've seen so many age gracefully, come out the penitentiary,
Within one year home they die.
I've seen the inside of the system also.
Time to read, think and write in a 7 by 3 solo.
Then I've been on the opposite side,
bail and bonds, we were young, so at times we got freed to our moms.
At other times life was just too hard,
reminiscing about the ones that went to god,
back to the essence.
This is the reason why I write.
I bleed life learning lessons.

Guardians

When I was young, I wasn't scared of the dark, I was scared of the shadows I saw in the evening's darkness, they would watch me. I became an insomniac staying up, waiting for them to attack. I swear I saw silhouettes of people; I just didn't know if they came in peace or were sent by evil. I wasn't taking a chance, I looked at waistlines instead of looking at their eyes just in case they had that medusa concrete glance or the power to hypnotize and leave me in a trance.

When I had sleepovers, I saw the shadows but didn't tell the others, they wouldn't believe what I see. As I got older, the shadows disappeared, but morning, noon and night, I felt the presence of some sort of entity, every hair strand on my body would stand, that's how I knew they were around me . . . Again, I didn't know if they were foe or friend, I just wondered when would it all end.

As a young man, the feeling still went on, by this time I knew they meant no harm . . . but who or what are they? Why did I see and feel them? Why do I now hear them? When I went left, they pulled right, when I was going to do wrong, they showed me the light, when I felt defeated, they spoke to me and told me . . . Inf, keep moving, all options aren't depleted.

Dead men from hustling past and my homies that returned to ash are who I saw felt and heard while I roamed blood bath aves, results of homicide became my guide, why? Because my experiences of sunshine and rain, hurt and pain when painted in verbal pictures with my pen will help end genocide, I didn't choose the life nor choose to write, I was chosen and was sent hell on earth protection.

Hard Days

Before my 13th birthday and on that 84 yay day, every day was earth day, I was packn it in like Green Bay. Massive cash is regular shit, interfere jugglers will have jugulars slit, Bellaco . . . On the road to the riches, you need a tight clique . . . That's rare like tight pussy and pretty clits. Inf has soldiers, all I gotta do is . . . point 'em out, point 'em out like hova, and it's ova. Yup, yup, it's the rice and bean eater, the recaito and sofrito bar mixer, that Manteca and perico trap life bleeder, like hip hops Red and Marley, I'm OG in the C and D arena. I'm from the days of holes in the walls, from spots in abandoned buildings that barely had stable stairs and floors, from the days where you were unbeatable if you had oowops at revolver times, ya know, 10's 11's and KG9's.

If ya didn't know the recipe you couldn't fuck with me, while I'm melting girl to a gooey gum, dudes were chopping 50/50 already done, I laughed sitting in a beach chair like I'm catching sun, watching them get tight at fiends coming back with clogged stems, my shit was pure and diesel, should've labeled slabs with boy g's obsession. Dudes bugged out if I let 'em see chefs' sessions, amazed they be like Inf's a crossover sensation, scratching their head they'll think . . . how did he come out with more than he put in the water, no wonder why his money is longer, I was out there putting work in getting time and a half on the corner.

I'm from New York

I'm from N.Y., a Yankee, an MVP like Derek G of C and D, I took the 6 like jlo, everybody but me was traveling, I was using mass transit transporting blow. I'm from a place that ain't safe even if you're a familiar face . . . Castle Hill . . . where kids kill kids and slugs fly at will with intentions on pushing back wigs. Lucrative traps led to living life with high stakes, mouth gags, blindfolds and duct tape for cake cake cake. I went to gun shows in the hood to cop extended clips with high grain ammo, went back to the hood and sold shells a dollar a bullet for low grain refills, I wasn't stupid, had to have the upper hand just in case we got into it. I kept tracers and beams for night war, went to the range to step up my aim for broad day gunplay protecting puntos from putos tryn to slow down my flow of ye. I was in the game so long my old connections are in homes with Alzheimer's, my first running mates got twenty plus years dead and in prison as lifers. I was in the game so long youngens started calling me mister when I was the youngest hustler calling pushers mister. I'm from the days of taj mahaj illusion vials, from the days of when I sat on my cellular and made calls with a coil wire connected to a receiver, from the days when Joey crack was the fat gangster, when chic was the emperor, when Paul was that nikka, from when George had an obsession, since Watson was first putting that inseparable familia together, there's too many to name, that block raised a lot of boss figures from the days of HP's wolf pack, nasty boys, Bryant boys, from the days of the wild cowboys, from the days I had Orlando my partner rip, he died in ninety one and I'm still reppn us my nikka. I stood behind holes in walls, in abandoned buildings with no ceilings and holes on floors, went to clubs to sell dubs of powder in bathroom stalls, then stepped up to a twelve-story crack mall . . . from then to now I saw noobs turn into veterans, veterans turn to dead men, I watched their children turn into noobs then veterans then dead men, a curriculum of generations becoming tenants in thug mansion. In my hood, if you ask a second child where's their big brother and father, it's a big chance that they'll point to the sky and say "with papa dios in heaven". I was running wild as a juvenile, trying reign supreme in Hell's Kitchen. Now as an older man, I mourn my friends and competition that passed trying to change poverty-stricken conditions, we all had one thing in common . . . that was get rich premonitions. I'm from N.Y., a Yankee, an MVP like Derek G of C and D.

Dreams

While at rest, I wish I could control the point and time my dreams would take place. I would dream of the late seventies and early eighties, just before eighty-four because up until that year, I had everybody with me. I'll be smiling while revisiting old fun times, like sitting in the back rear facing seat in dad's Brady bunch station wagon with the wood trim paneling, playn punch car alone, I punched myself when I saw a buggy Volkswagen while traveling to get bean soup or bean pie from the brothers in Harlem wearing suits with bow ties. I would sit in that same seat with the entire family on 95 to cross the George Washington bridge then to the palisades with a motorcade of his people, we're heading to the seven lakes, on a Sunday it was like little Puerto Rico. Grown folk on one side doing what grown folk do, a lot of brews, a joint or two, dancing till they're sweaty, hatch backs open, eight tracks playing, it was usually el gran combo or Ruben blades blaring from radios. The kids did what kids do . . . feast, we had all you can eat arroz con pollo, coca cola or Pepsi had us ping ponging all over, we had to wait till later in the day for grandmothers with big oyas on a grill or over a campfire to make outdoor sopa, until then we swam and played then get upset when we heard "it's time to go", that was the life to us ghetto kids we never wanted it to be over. I miss my dad. Good ole times, good ole times. I loved those trips.

In those same years, I had all my peers . . . (the sound of a can full of rocks hitting the ground) rattattat, I see Ralphy behind that old abandoned duster, rattattat, I see you behind that tree, come out Edgar. While searching for my other friends, I see Orlando running his fast ass to kick that can, he got there before me and kicked it far, now I gotta start from scratch looking for them behind trees and cars. We played round-up, man-hunt, snuck into Jamie towers and played all sharks under, we turned off the lights in elevators, went up and down swinging wild, playing corners, dudes came out with nose bleeds, busted lips and black eyes . . . we played rough-touch in the middle of the street dogging traffic, we played whiffle ball, sponge ball, hardball, football basketball, scratching tops and bottoms off sturdy cans to aim hydrant water at each other was usually how we ended it all after having a ball . . . that's a good day hanging with the guys. A beautiful dream. After eighty-four dreams turned into nightmares, dad dies, we fall victim to poverty, there went those one on one and family trips. A lot of my friends kicked the can, some became reasons for manhunts until they got rounded up, we can no longer play all sharks under, cause dudes went to jail or are buried six feet under, days ended getting sprayed, not by hydrant water but by killers' fingers squeezing triggers.

A Donor with Limitations

When I die, I'm going to do others a favor because I signed my license as a donor, I won't be selfish. Use any part of my body, recycle my anatomy. My death will help others live. Time will be of the essence in preventing others from returning to it, so rush me into the o.r. so docs can start to dissect and reconnect moments after I listen to the fat lady's music.

Somebody on dialysis could use my kidneys, somebody with emphysema can use my lungs, someone with a bad heart slowly dying can receive the heart of a lion. There's only one thing I refuse to share. My eyes. I'm going to ask my family to seal 'em shut although they'll be closed already, glue them and label them "bad for your health". I don't want my visions to be viewed by anyone, I wouldn't wish that on my worst enemy, nevertheless to someone that just wishes for twenty twenty.

Hurt and pain isn't something that's only felt, it also can be seen, looking through my eyes will cause instant insanity, I mean people will actually pull out their hair witnessing my daymares or commit suicide for watching my nightdreams. You can't use dark glasses or patches to cover what you're seeing because my retinas work as recorders and they'll play them over and over till tear ducts start bleeding, flashes of death will occur, causing them to randomly start screaming.

They'll see bullet holes, stab wounds and self-inflicted wounds, they'll see a bunch of kids cross over shortly after coming out their mother's womb, at times they'll lose focus and fall into deep stares looking at all the parents that are left to live in despair . . . Letting somebody see what I've seen just wouldn't be fair, chop me up, freeze what needs to be frozen, but please leave my eyes in my skeleton.

It's Showtime

It's showtime. The names introduced . . . Infinite the poet. Here comes the truth, I step to the stage and flip through my book of rhymes in my mind . . . which ones will it be . . . they come to me . . . I begin with the poetry. I go hard whether it's a crowd of seventh graders or a platform full of slammers . . . no filter. Capturing attention off the jump is my goal, the damns, wow, the lumpy throats and eyes getting teary let me know they feel me, I am thankful for that because reliving tragedies takes its toll. I get in my b boy stance and go into a stanza trance; my regulars quote my signature when I quote my signature but in a whisper. When I spit new pieces, it's a dead silence, even the breathing ceases . . . everybody knows I'm the bad boy as if Sean signed me, not cause of my personality but because of my unorthodox style of urban poetry. I get it in. I'm from the bx born and raised, the all-mighty dollar says in God we trust like a sacred verse so like Jesus and Allah it was praised, bodies lowered and souls lifted as it rained for three days, crime pays, the price is life. I explain that verbally after memorizing the written pain when I remove pen caps.

The Urban Bar

I don't get at cats cause I'll give 'em fame, cats don't get at me because I spit flame, lyrically and physically when I aim. I been takn it easy educating the youth, once and a while I have to remove the filter and show I'm the truth. My thoughts derive from the birth of the hard circa, ya know the kill or be killed eighty to 2G era, to reign supreme you had to have power and be clever, if not for three days your area would have bad weather, pain rain from led showers will drench mourners. Power . . . I have it and don't abuse it, cleverness . . . I did dirt with cleanliness; nothing was ever personal it was all business. Inf was safe in the paint cause while roaming Hell's Kitchen, I wore Cubans that stood on statues' necks being blessed by saints.

I got hit, while laying on a gurney with a fifty-fifty chance to see the pearlies. Momma handed me a crucifix, but I wasn't done learning urban poetry, so as soon as the stitching and broken bones healed, I was back in the bricks. Cast, cane, gat, caine Tylenol with codeine to ease the pain. I recouped . . . that's how it supposed to be, but it didn't turn out that way for branches of the tree, it was as if all year long was autumn, my codees dropped like leaves cause of redrum, cash ruled everything around me like the acronym, if money is the root of all evil . . . I had flame retardant rubber bands around satan. Homicide after homicide I continued to ride, I was in the mind state of . . . why live, if I have more people on the other side?

The new generation came up and blew. In the matter of a few years, I would have to empty out a keg of beer for the dead cause they died too, I'm going to cemetery after cemetery to clean then kiss headstones of two generations of the bellaco crew, pause . . . I loved dudes that never made it out gauze.

Albert 'Infinite the Poet' Carrasco

Head shots, stab wounds and self-inflictions are the reason why when I grab a pen, I lay it down in critical condition

Forgive Us

We are not bad. We've sinned over and over and probably will sin again to get a grasp on what never had, but again I say . . . we are not bad. Before there were choices there were only options, those options were to try succeed by any means necessary or settle for less and quickly regress to a position worse than what we are living in already. Believe me, a lot of us screamed out for help but those screams were ignored like careless whispers, but our actions always got attention. Some rob and steal, push weight and squeeze steel just for at least one steady daily meal, others will do the same but just to see how being rich feels. Growing up in the projects, there weren't outlets other than the streets, black markets. We became peddlers of powder like our forefathers. Sometimes us juveniles were on the block for hours together with never made it but still trying seniors, they figure that they're breathing, so there's still opportunity to not be considered failures. If you were to ask any of us that was mentioned above if we liked what we were doing, we would all say no. It's just that we did bad good so the hatred for it didn't show. You know how excited I was when I got my first job? I was so excited that I had to tell all my friends about it. So, I went to the cemetery with urns so I can tell them all at once, that I found a way to legally earn. Forgive us for our sins, all we wanted to do was bread win.

Albert 'Infinite the Poet' Carrasco

Mental Movies

I have cinematic visions of street wars, bloody gurneys and men laying in critical condition with bodily fluids leaking through limb and head wrapped gauze. My past is the director and my mind is the illustrator . . . there's no actors, but in the credits, there's many characters. They can be seen engraved over the braves' graves. I screamed "cut" years ago, but life kept filming men ready to die for money, power and respect and they kept dying at an alarming rate trying to get families off welfare and out the projects. I never wanted to see what it looked like inside torsos and my homies' heads, but I saw it, so I see red, I see rigor mortis, I hear ad-libs of the dead. Visual scripts are encrypted in my cerebellum. When played out, they become urban poetry in motion.

No In-between

Blood rushes when guns bust for that in God we trust by boy and girl money lushes. It's ER visits for stepped on eina or low number rated her-on. The streets are filled with hungry felon repeaters, the arena isn't made for every get rich-dreamer, it's controlled by seniors that were born into the life as misdemeanors. Connections retire or die, boss men become connections, capos become bosses, pitchers become capos . . . hustler evolution. In NY, it's easy to become a john for stepping on toes, you'll just be a body bleeding profusely that none of the dough boys know, they'll all be mad though, a corpse on a get money block is a no no, cause for a few days, homicide investigations slow up that cop and go flow, the hitters will get a pass when they explain that he was a fiend snatching Fulano, they'll get hit off to take off and avoid the fuego. You can't just wake up one day and say . . . I'm going to open up shop . . . cause shells will drop before the cutthroats finished their first copp. You gotta get put on or be born in the life . . . No in-between when it comes to street cream.

The Underdog

I learnt everything in life through trial and error, the odds would be stacked up against me, I would still try to climb over, I taught myself to understand that failure was the first steps to success, so I failed over and over until I mastered movements, life to me was like chess. Through every loss and defeat, I gained experience, knowledge, education. That's why on my final lap in situations, I remembered how I was trapped, knew how to react, made quick decisions to make precise evasions . . . losing so much, I became a veteran. I'm a goal chaser like the reaper is the soul chaser. I will not give up. Anything I target, I pursue till I have a lock on it as if I'm chasing a Charlie after taking off from a carrier by the navy as a fighter pilot. I was told I will always be poor, so I tried not to be, they said I would die, so I roamed no man's land cautiously, people told me I would never amount to nothing, those same people now show courtesy due to false assumptions and pre-judging me. Don't let people cover your ideas, thoughts or motivation with an invisible gray cloud, follow your dreams no matter how long it takes to get there, because when you do emerge from the shroud after being told you'll never do so by haters and naysayers, you'll feel extra proud.

I'm from a Place

I'm from a place where you can get rich quickly or become a memory just as fast, ya know like when you drive by cemeteries or walk through your house looking at urns every time you pass. Ain't nothn sweet 'bout the bricks, it's not a place to raise children but some are forced too to make ends meet assisted by EBT and wic.

The only thing that'll ever change about the game is the players, that's pure facts, after I retired, youngens I used to send to the store for a Dutch and a Pepsi with extra money to see if they're trustworthy are now doing the same to another shorty's in the trap. It's tradition. Me and a bunch of brothers were store runners that became block owners when deed holders got sent up, become users or a statistic of murder.

We had a steroid flow with perico like we were in the point, the bully and watson pushing diesel, ole g's planted it but we benefited off the root of all evil . . . blood currency from sales of dimes and nickels, I said dimes first cause if you didn't have ten, we'll break it in half and bump ya a nickel. The new generation became hustln sensations with boy g obsessions, our run was a good one, I can't lie . . . that was because at the time no one had yet to die.

They say it rains for three days when someone dies, if that was true there would've been so much water that I would've had to build an arc like Noah after the reaper came for my crew. Back-to-back fam got wet in the trap, holes in heads, holes in torsos, every year there was less and less bellacos, the circle got smaller but tighter, anybody about that life knows how it goes.

Vintage BX

Infinite is vintage bx, OG like snoop d o double g in the projects, an ex-Raekwon with the Pyrex, an ex-bail and bonder, safe house owner for absconders especially if you were on my team tryn to move comas over. I was known for having military intelligence, military ordinance, for govern'n with fear over love like the prince and that was in my years of adolescence. I rolled with bosses before they knew so, like orlandito a representa of bellaco, and a lot of other Spanish good fellas that rolled like mike Vic's pits, salivating like kugo, trying to get money like menudo. I showed my pañas and manitos in the rotten manzana that us Latinos have power like tainos as I knocked them rectangles down like dominoes. I was caught up in the revolution of dead men, I became them, I just went through evolution cause I was lucky to continue breathn.

Children from my era tried to be kings but died young like tutankhamun, not from malaria but because of murder. I'm destroying what my forefathers created and what I followed, so these young ride or die cats don't become headless equestrians like the sleepy hollow legend. See . . . I'm a crack baby. Mama didn't abuse narcotics. I was just a baby selling crack running from narcotics, now, a few decades later I'm the crack man, an urban spoken prospect, a narrator of the life of illegal profit, a lyrical savior preventing friends and family from attending impromptu all black affairs.

Danger

From a place where children can come outside at any given time of the day, look on the floor for heroin discarded syringes and act like they're doctors and patients as they dangerously role-play without knowing the danger of contracting deadly diseases. They're only trying to pass time, not trying to be spoken of in past time. I'm from a place where you can walk the neighborhood and collect so many assorted color and size slabs that if we were to recycle them, we'll make a few rainbow boxes of hefty bags. I'm from a place where it could be summer time but there's no sunshine. It's just a season of bright light and heat melting tar-paved streets. Where winter is just the same . . . cold as summer. Where I'm from, parents go through daily dejavu, todays and tomorrows are just like yesterday to them, hustling worrying about how they'll feed their hungry family when "what's for dinner" is an unanswerable question. I'm from a place where sons and fathers get stopped and frisked together and as long as they live in the hood, they'll fit the stereotypical description forever to the outsider overseers. If I were to walk block to block and gather all the spent cartridges of all the attempt and murders and place them side by side, they'll exceed the span of any of the New York bridges.

The Worst Was the Best

The worst thing that happens to me was the best thing that happened to me, I'm a reaction to actions, I am destiny. In seventy-one, mom gave birth to a son that'll be known for his urban tongue, little did she know she'll have to raise my brothers and I in poverty because we lost the breadwinner of the family. Before the breadwinner died, I learnt the ropes, Infinite is a hustler's son, I was raised around sales of raw and observed the slurred speech and crooked jaws, I saw sales of doo-G and observed the raspy voice and the constant need to avoid the monkey, I witnessed the sales of tystick and observed the red eyes and the . . . What was I going to say? . . . Memory loss from those making it look like Woodstock in the bricks. I was lucky . . . It all was preparation. Oppression lead me to connections, I connected with them, I had nothing, they made donations, needed to make a dollar from a quarter, so I pushed weed, boy and girl powder with the fellas, My house was broken, so I used the streets to mend it together, just like the glue used on my teammates eyes and lips to keep them shut after every murder, just like charges . . . before getting peeled off by retainers, just like the bullet stuck by my lung that was too close for an operation that remains as a reminder. When it rained, it poured . . . I was a pour bearer, when slugs rained, blood poured, I carry flesh and bone, hurt and pain, I'm a pallbearer, what didn't break me, made me mentally stronger, when I spit, I bring life to water, I'm not going to feed you lies or glamorize, I'll let them fiction writers spit stillborn Protozoa, my past made me a face of urban poetry and title of a nonfiction urban author.

Urban Preaching

Yeah, your name is ringing 'round town, you're idolized, not only do the hustlers and freaks hear and see ya shining, so do police.

Believe me, it's gonna be bars or belts lowering you six feet down when you're deceased.

I'm a prime example of the life of pure rectangles and arsenals, clips full of mistletoes, mothers give foreheads the kiss of death when it's time for her sons to go, after the guns blow.

I lived the life of les miserables, youths in montifore or Jacobi laid in critical. . . in this life, death is typical, blood-soaked gauze is topical when slugs enter and ricochet in you.

I was that shorty rocking jewelry all gaudy, I was the one popping off on impulse, no warnings, why, cause I was shot up and was tired of homie mourning and praying to old dead homies to let them know another homie is coming.

In housing authority, my block was untouchable. I was the Teflon don of a housing lobby before position was given to gotti.

Money stacked on money, too much to count, didn't have a money machine so I weighed my residuals on triple beam residue, I multiplied bills by the face of the image of man, didn't matter, 1s, 5s, 10s, 20s grants and benjis, every bill weighed a gram.

Albert 'Infinite the Poet' Carrasco

I manipulated powder to form rocks with soda water and pyrex pots. My monopolizing brothers cultivate soil under marble plots.

I lost so many close to me, feels like every other day is another dead friends' yearly anniversary.

I rolled alongside the best, a lot of dudes thirty years later are now homeless, they thought the game would last forever, now they're at a dead-end, no funds, friends and people looking up to them, in fact the ones that did, got older and walk right past when they see the one they idolize with their hand out asking for quarters.

It's effed up how at times I see older men with no direction, their rap sheet goes back to adolescent incarceration, youthful offending, rejected resumes have some thinking life after that life has no meaning, treatment by employers and others is demeaning.

Listen youngens, I banged, I slang, I carpe diem, carved them, slabbed them, saw coroners bag men of my team, I lived that dream and woke up to a nightmare, at times I relive the past through deep thought in blank stares, I cry tearless tears internally for the peers I've lost for an eternity. I beg that I don't catch Alzheimer's for constantly thinking of my old time pañas that I knew since foot-fitting pajamas and sleepovers, now my face causes mothers to weep in remembrance of my brother that is forever asleep, not because they hate me, they just remember when we were kids, wearing pajamas with feet, innocent souls with no worries, sporting smiles as we sleep.

Grinding

I'm out here, grind'n through sleepless nights and unrestful days, writing and reciting, pushing my pen work like yay, I scribe 1000 words about the life and times of bellaco, copy write it, then flip it to the prices of today's kilos, then do it again and again, I'm sitting on mad material, so I became a trap connection. I listen to the radio and nod my head to the lies of imaginary gangsters because it's entertainment, all I pay attention to is hooks and beats because most tracks lack lyricism. Think about this . . . if you're 100 kids' favorite spitter and your rhymes about street life start and end as if everybody can be a winner . . . what are you doing to them? I give it up raw like cocaine when it's pure, so the youth can hear the truth on what's in store if they make a spot by the store pushing cooked and pure. You can make a million . . . it's true. You can drive expensive cars . . . it's true. You can travel the world . . . it's true. In-between, there's things usually kept out of view like raids, men in the yard and lots of marble slabs representing those that returned to God . . . I fill in trap gaps with facts. I remember being on foreign islands, spending thousands screaming out "we made it". I remember looking through morgue windows at those that sat at the table with me with a tube here and a cut there . . . they didn't make it.

Got It Bad

Fiends searching for money to twist a slab . . . I try to push it to the side and do something regular but I keep thinking about it, it calls me, I gotta habit, I must have it, every binge I get higher. There's no rehab for my addiction and no detox for my actions, I just take hits all day long, giving the monkey on my back satisfaction. I travel place to place, borough to borough, state to state, sharing what I abuse, I'm yo pusha, I'll be your first drug introducer, my goal is to have the world strung out on what I use and deliver. The young world is my target. I know if I get them early, there's no way they'll be able to avoid me, I go to schools when the auditorium is full like assembly and give them all something for free and because of me, a few of them will grow up and be other than what they would be without me . . . I am a "bad" influence . . . the substance I abuse needs no pity, I guess, I'll infinitely be a manufacturer and deliverer of urban poetry.

The Hustle

The game ended, not the struggle. My presence isn't present cause I'm hustling "infinite". Sorry, fam and friends, I still have hunger, I'm eager and I'm not getting younger, my time is monopolized by writing and memorizing rhymes to educate the blind with masterpieces of my mind. I stand in the trap and manufacture pure crack in my cerebellum, I gotta be careful not to catch the Rico act for producing crack verbalism. I'm already known for being a hood heroin, a hard knock veteran of Coke and her-ron, cause if I wasn't over the stove, I was gettn that table grind on, I use that buzz to do what it does, to prevent all black affairs while releasing doves and to prevent kites being sent to those we love. I sacrifice all recreational to write words so influential and detrimental for those that are constantly being cuffed and hauled off to central. book me to keep the bookings empty, incarcerate yourself in my bars, do daily bids to my poetry, you can do it at home personally instead of searching for crime loopholes with others at the law library. See, I'm a survivor of misery and terror, so I'm reaching my hand back into the fire to lift up tradition followers, I was them, they are me, my forefathers didn't educate me, they taught me mixtures and recipes, I teach the reasons why bullet holes are on my body and why I'm still waiting for dudes to come home from the eighties. My forefathers died rich, I thought I would too but it didn't work out that way, I lived longer, went up and down like a yo yo dealing with yeyo, went through raids, wars and constant body lowering ceremonies . . . ain't that a bitch? This is drug prevention education from the lemniscate in the vicinity of district 8.

Lived and Learned

People say . . . Inf, I didn't know you could spit like that; I say, me neither, but since I really lived most of my life surrounded by traps dealn crack it's natural to produce ether. I witnessed it all . . .

How it is to ball . . . Foreign whips, strictly 50s and 100s in money clips, trips on planes and ships, buying out bars to open a bottle and take a sip to wet my lips before turning the night to free drinks for all the chics . . . that's giving back to the community from chips made from lucrative strips.

How it is to fall . . . Sitting at the top melting kelos after kelo in Pyrex pots went to more soda than regular to blow up seven grams in an empty jelly jar. Hustln for profit turned over, now I'm hustln for freedom . . . bail, bond and lawyers. I'm walkn around with my stomach touchn my back, I have a pocket full of scrilla but I had to decide whether I eat or make sure I have that rent, car note and monthly charge for those retainers . . . that's a no-brainer . . . I just kept telln myself, I'll eat later, when it was time for breakfast, lunch and dinner.

How it is to get jail calls . . . Yo, Inf, so and so got knocked, they caught him with the glock, Inf, mo got caught on the ave with the pack instead of putting it in the stash, Inf, shorty got bagged in ye crib in Broadway. On the road to the riches, there were bars, I even got my mom arrested and put in rikers . . . imagine that scar. From just a judge roast, it went to homes, spofford, then prisons all around the east coast. I broke night with peers that had to turn in that morning to do years, I've been writing lines for those that got caught for white crime and sending them in kites since stamps were just a dime.

How it is to get death calls . . . Ring ring, hello? . . . Inffffff, (sobbing) he's dead! Who did it, how did it happen, where is he? The Q and A automatically begins, this happened over and over, ring ring . . . there goes another brother, becoming a statistic of murder. I got calls from homies, angry, telln me another homie died, mothers calling, crying, telln me their son died, fathers calling me, enraged, telling me when and where to take revenge for junior . . . sons and daughters were too young to understand, so they ask me . . . where's my daddy? I wish there was no cellulars, that way I could've remembered my men alive a little longer. This is why when I spit about the façade, you see it clearer.

Had to Have It

I woke up early or broke night to make sure I was first on the strip to get this money, there was a demand, so I kept bundles and grams for those that needed a blast to open them up or to control or remove that monkey . . . I'm following tradition. I want to eat daily, want jewels, a house and cars, I'll deal with hurt, I'll suppress the pain, I understand the game, so be it if I have to gain inner and outer scars.

I'm shouting out my color, when I see fiends walking in the wrong direction, it's a cut throat hustle, I called it interceptions. Dudes use to stomp and threaten customers, that's how it was easy to steal sales, I'll give samples and take shorts to build clientele. After a while, it was word of mouth . . . go see bori, he's on the come up and he got it good, I just fell back and dealt with lines for boy and girl in the hood.

It's a wrap, I'm on the road to the riches like cool g rap, had to make sure the last re dried before I bumped the last pack. A major rule . . . never have an empty trap, while I chopped squares, there was a pitcher there to make sure there's no gaps. Ayo shorty, I like how you get down, take my number, if your people don't have it, call me, I'm always around, Infinite, fuck with me, my prices are lower, bellaco, give me a try, you'll see I got that butta, BX, Harlem, the heights, alphabet city, BK offers are coming from all over. I was just a juvenile; the buzz went international as I got older.

Was in a position to put my fam on, so I did, I scouted others searching for the best of the best by watching their movements, it was like they were blind auditioning for da kid. Whoever I liked, got upgraded, I'll pull up and make 'em made men, now we're crime related, boy and girl affiliated, before life sentences and mass murder . . . I thought, we all made it.

Stage 8

When it comes to the streets, I go hard rep'n my fam that went back to God and those in the yard, Inf's the epitome of the beast belly, I was there very long, living blasphemous, I'm still there but now I'm stage "8", lyrically cancerous, the game is gonna need an oncologist cause everything you heard before me is benign, they're behind, it's my time to kill the beast with malignant rhymes. My poetry is gonna make the illuminati want to merk me like they did to willy because of our science when we polly, every story that's told sets back population control, the more I'm read or heard, they'll be less souls sold and less bodies stiff around blood puddles after blowing out nose blood bubbles cause of slugs that entered torsos and heads. The streets aren't sweet, while trying to make ends meet, shotas made it rain slugs that hit my thugs in this cold world like hail and sleet. We got money, whenever punani, every day was a party, it felt like as if every year we were burying a homie, vayas con dios, after burials we went right back, medicating fiends with a nickel, dime or dub dose. Being a survivor of a lifestyle in which many died makes me an experienced mourning griot, the bx, home of the brave and early graves, in the house that Coke built, my pitch will get me the most saves.

He Wanted In!

I wanted to be down with them so bad that I used to beg them please, they had all the women, money, power and respect, I sold the drugs but was too scared to squeeze. To be recognized by them I had to commit the ultimate sin and I really wanted to be "in". The next opportunity I got to prove myself, I proved my worth by closing my eyes, pulln the trigger and eliminating targets or competition. I was scared of death lookn at a face of death . . . that was the beginning. It was hard to shake off the nervousness and harder listening to my conscious . . . what are you doing? Thou shall not kill, what are you proving? . . . The process is ill. It's okay tho, now I'm down with a set, they call me wife B cause I leave them white tee's wet, I've gotten used to it . . . I no longer close my eyes when I squeeze, shit, I'll murder for rec, fame and hits, if I have to kill for what I love, so be it . . . There's going to be mass releasing of doves, and the streets are going to be filled with sheets absorbing blood like a cotex on a period. I didn't want to become evil, all I wanted was to live like rich men did . . . no worries and tranquil. For wanting to be a part of a league of extraordinary men, I'll be roaming hell's surface forever because there's no room for what I've become in heaven.

Lost Bail

I could live wealthy for the rest of my life, if the city would return all of my lost bail due to dudes catching new charges, or teammates not showing up to court on sentencing day, laying low in screaming out "fuck jail". Just gettn ten percent, my bondsman in Brooklyn definitely made a million . . . retainers . . . from beginning to ending, definitely made millions. It was all well worth it regardless to the fact I can't get that back, it's all lost profit. Let me tell ya about more losses in the life of crime bosses . . . we were at the table racking up eight balls in our younger years, we didn't know there was a difference between chefn and sniffn, so we wondered why when we tried to turn straight nose candy over it would disappear. Pyrex cracked, leaving stove tops with half-cooked ready rock until we learnt how to double boil, so if the pyrex cracked, the process could continue in a rusty tin pot. Let me get deeper. About a key was lost from narcs eyeballing bombs, they had us running from our projects to other complexes like a freedom marathon . . . cause if they caught us, our ass was gone.

Lucky

Lucky, I ain't on the shit I used to be on, cause when I spit, it wasn't poetry . . . it was trips to triage and emergency at Jacobi, Montifore or bronx Lebanon. I evolved, left the game of guns, coke and her-on, now the drug I hustle to cause addiction is urban apostrophe and my voice is my weapon. I pop off on the regular on social media, in schools . . . I gotta give consignment to the future . . . in the hood to misdemeanors that are raised by the actions of predicate fast life repeaters and in any spot they want me to feature and carpe diem, seize the day with urban wordplay. My nonfiction narrations of the streets are education; I use lessons of self-destruction, so others can go through reconstruction before they burn on the surface of hell . . . spontaneous combustion. We all wanted the same thing, that was to get out of poverty and live wealthy. That didn't happen for many, unfortunately they helped build blocks but died before they could taste the money. Their blood shed, tears and incarcerated years was just so whoever was next for position could eat a little better, so on and so forth, the game didn't change, just new players started where the old ones left off. I retired, now I'm like a scout looking for players to pull out the fire.

Phle-body-me

I spit death because I lived to talk about it. I was a teen living in the devil's mezzanine, all the murders I've seen makes my vision red like infrared beams, I have daymares and night dreams because my past life of feeding fiends. I see my men, then I see redrum, then I see and hear yelling from corpses that went through rigor mortis, I wish my retinaes didn't record this, I wish my mind didn't remember seeing my friends with an infinite scream, cause those are the scenes that'll replay in my head over and over, forever.

After being my brother's keeper, I went to being a soul searcher screaming out to my kin "one day, we'll meet up again, I'll find ya, my brothers". Until then, I'll use my mouth, keyboards, pencils and ballpoint pens as an urban poetic medium. My mind is like a planchette, words appear on paper like a ouija board when I translate what the dead said.

I gather an audience to have a spoken seance. I'll contact the crossed-over like an Indian chief calling onto spirits, so they can use me to spread wisdom and guidance to the future from the essence. At times, I hear "let me speak", "Infinite, tell my story". There're people on the other side anxious to explain to the world why and how they died to prevent similar drug-life homicides. Every day, it's the same scenario, I see and converse with the no longer-living, hustlers like a male urban spoken version of Theresa caputo.

Summer Nights

The hood ain't the same, not too long ago in the summer at night, peeps were drinkn nutcrackers and nemos, playn dominoes, shootn dice . . . 456 celo, gutting gars and puff puff passing to the circle, everybody is fresh to death like the diplos, the bitty in the big park in chp was a lounge like the 40/40, everyone that came thru was vip, the only rules were byobud aint no cheeba hawks round here, homie. Ole timers would be leaning on pillows, smokn square after square, looking out the window, peeps from li the q boro bk and harlem pulled up on Randall, making the strip look like a car show. We would spontaneously bounce to the seaport, coney island, AC or jersey shore . . . seaside heights preferably, if it wasn't raining, it was a party. Clubs, after hours, the beach then repeat the next day in that same order. Sometimes we packed can goods, toilet paper, flashlights, tents, and drove out the hood to break a few nights in bear-mountains woods. What happened to the good ole summer nights?

Listen

I told 'em so, but they ain't listen, I warned 'em but they chose to do them, I'm no know-it-all, I just made mistakes and corrected them, I also witnessed the errors of many men, my knowledge from experience is > than the average, when I speak uncommon sense, it comes out like a different language, their norm dialect is nonsense. We all want to come up, how we go about it makes a difference, I polled with men that wanted to take it all over like scar, I told 'em I hear ya but I rather start my own and become the trap life bar. Young Bellaco was taught by men with no ego, Al, you can get rich but the path to success is deadly, life became more and more of a bitch when a narrow ditch becomes home to another homie. It's bad enough we shit where we sleep, don't leave bodies in the street and make sure all your homies eat, don't be flashy and use the cover of night to creep. Cats weren't on bellaco's level, to c our currency you had to go o.t. and bubble, da flow was sicker than a combination of NC, SC, Newburgh and Monticello, we were the sticks in the bricks, everybody else was under us like they're playing limbo, they had lil' nickels while we had two for five boulders, the same size of the dice, we tossed to play celo. I try to teach these youngens facts like the ogees taught me in the pursuit of the root of all evil, I tell the bad with the good, keeping reality back ain't really hood. The reaction to those actions was drama with corrections at visitations and forehead-kissing of my kin, frozen after passing. I went through it all to ball, I explained it to many men, they didn't listen, I warned 'em but they chose to do them, the streets remained the same what changes is tradition to a new generation . . . Infinite is here to make a deception interception.

You're Welcome

I saved many lives by just being at the right place at the right time, being affiliated with bosses and marksmen prevented dudes' fam from hearing the death tone when they flatline, my presence granted pardons, alright Inf, we'll let him live but you owe me one . . . so, I did the same for them when I was around and it was going to be their turn to succumb to the gun. Real respected real, so if a target is around me, their drama is my drama and nobody wanted to get flanked by concrete soldiers . . . besides, dudes wasn't really ready for war, if they didn't listen and go in, it was like violating the Geneva convention, one by one their entire team would wind up in ER's in critical condition, if two were found together it was a twin funeral procession, three or more went to thug mansion together through the buddy system, or everybody at one time at a reunion or some sort of get-together and celebration. Power was mine but I didn't abuse it unless it was preventing a re-run of that fat lady's music. The underdogs loved me . . . I over stand that all hustlers are on the food chain in the game but I've felt so much hurt that I hate to see others feel pain. I put guys I knew wouldn't make it on their own under my wing, protected og's when their names would no longer ring, I was raised to want for others as want for myself . . . I wanted to live wealthy, so for them, I wanted the same thing, it's a competition arena, I'll beat my comp without things getting bloody, then give 'em an opportunity to join me, they didn't have to be full of envy or become enemies, they could become small cells scattered all over from the bellaco army. If there was no kill'n, everybody would've made millions, I'm not saying the streets was good for us, what I'm saying is I made the streets less dangerous as we lived blasphemous on hell's surface.

Albert 'Infinite the Poet' Carrasco

Tomorrow

I've always anticipated tomorrows because my todays were filled with sadness and sorrow. Willing to let the happenings of right now marinate till a later time was how I played tricks on my mind. When rent was late, I told momma, don't worry, tomorrow we'll get it straight, when there was nothing to eat, I thought about yesterday and what I ate saying to myself its ok, its ok, tomorrow, we'll have rice beans and steak, then I'd say the same thing the next day, looking at a dinner-less plate. I wouldn't dwell on facing starvation or going through the embarrassment of eviction, I would tell myself one of these days ahead will bring a solution to yesterday's trials and tribulations. Today isn't final, if I'm alive for the next day. I had surplus amounts of hope, that's how I coped, facing defeat, I still wouldn't throw in the towel, I just re-strategized then re-orchestrated a new plan for tomorrow. What came after momma's water bag broke, and before the placenta was a go-getter, from day one, struggles were placed at my feet, I knew the type of obstacles that were in store, I had to wait a few tomorrows to gain weight if I wanted to leave those hospital doors after being born premature. Yesterdays are experiences, tomorrows are new beginnings to me, what shall they be? . . . I'll just have to wake up the next day, and I shall see.

My Home

The benches were my living room, the park activity was my TV, it had surround-sound of reality, switching channels was looking in different directions, everything was live, no reruns or commercial interruptions. I used my finger and park house water to brush my teeth, my boxers are stuck to my ass, my socks are stuck to my feet, I have bags under my eyes because of lack of sleep. I'm binge-blazing L's for breakfast lunch and dinner, trying to eat in these bx streets. My look was horrid, I'm scruffy, my jeans are dirty but pockets were filthy, I didn't want to leave the ave to shave, shower and change, feeling ill be losing cash, I'm tryn to add not subtract math, so I'll be in the living room where men die as days pass. In the winter, my hoodie was a sheet, my coat was a quilt, and a garbage can full of twigs and branches lit on fire was my heat. In the summer, those benches worked like hammocks, since my living room didn't have a roof, at night I looked through the smog to stare at the stars as if I was in the Caribbean on vacation. In autumn, I watched leaves fall, in the spring, I was still on that park bench trying to ball. I had running mates . . . oooops, my bad, roommates, but they relocated to heaven . . . they became the "late".

Woodwind and Brass

Infinite used to be in school auditoriums playing woodwind and brass, I could have been a musician, but instruments got pushed to the side for faces on thin sheets of wood while I was caught up with a Pyrex glass, instead of being an industry rock star, Albertito became an in-da-street rock star, chefn then choppn boulders with single edge gemstars. Music notes turned to c notes, I failed my music teacher mr. renaldini trying to escape poverty's clutches like a hustling Houdini, the game wasn't me. If you asked what I wanted to do when I grew up, my reply would be a "soldier in the military", not an advertiser of eight balls, two for five or one for three, I never made it to boot camp, but I did enlist in the streets and made a trap for staying stationary after giving out samps and hoping they came back with change, cash or food stamps. I stood at attention, couldn't be at ease cause of d's and watchn bombs before they get swiped by stash thieves. Innocence turned to me, pleading it every time I got caught in the park or projects, bumpn powder or bass hits. Every day the sun rose and fell, I was sucked deeper and deeper into hell, I was good but because of the way I was living, you couldn't tell, I looked hood with no laces on timbs, no belt on fatigues and no string in my hood . . . that was just my ensemble to scramble and so I didn't have to take nothing off in processing cells, I could've been a famous percussionist instead I became infamous for drug sales, three facades later I became a poet that holds weight-like scales, I graduated hard knocks magnum cum laude, so I carpe diem with militant wordplay.

Feel It in the Air

I felt it in the air, I have a heightened sense of awareness. Mannerisms set off alarms, they alert me of intent of bodily harm. Why is he asking for forgiveness? If I can't remove myself outta harm . . . blam blam blam, better you than me, somebody's getting the business. I wish I could've been here and there to feel it in the air, but I couldn't, so I mourn.

I was chefn, resting, sexing, block to block first and second chirping, stack counting, blazing, partying and bullshitting, when I got nine elevens from the days of beepers to the new millennium after hitters bodied my men. It's a never-ending hard feeling knowing my homies was hit up bleeding while I was in the kitchen, laid up, in guts, in bucks short shifting, PC splitting and THC inhaling while fast life celebrating.

Every man bleeds the same, I'm not bulletproof, the burn holes on my skin and the slug in my chest is proof, lucky that three days later, I didn't get a rock with a death date under my name, every day after I studied the art of war while remaining a hard knock valedictorian of raw, I became a street life veteran and learnt more and more through every tour, survival mode went on automatically as soon as I walked out my project door.

Mic Sex

We put it down! See, I, a manly man, so, of course she bust first. I'm looking and mm mmm mmmm listening to her talk nasty, she went in, like "next", she made it hard for me. In my mind I'm say'n . . . okay okay, this woman ain't play'n, her head game is amaz'n. When it's my turn, imma show her how I spit shine but for now, I keep lett'n her seduce me before I go for mine.

She's in the zone sweat'n, she isn't a thot but she's known what she's doing because she's dropp'n it like it's hot . . . am I feel'n her? No question, the girl is a problem. She knows her game is cray cray, when she got her nut off, she looked at me so so so sexy like . . . it's your turn playa, play.

I got on it quickly, whatever I touch gets wet instantly, right out the gate I ate, I could her say'n damn baby, I'm look'n at her . . . hush hush, like sizzla, got her attention then went harder, um um hun, Inf ain't tak'n one for the cru, she kept quiet but was bitt'n her lip like h o l y shit . . . she loves what I do. I'm tak'n her there, I see her face of excitement while I go behind her and get it in as if I'm violent, she can't take it, damn fam, you make me feel like a virgin, I nutted then said, na, you're a spitta's dream, you're a ten, she said . . . this right here is something I needed, when can we do it again? I said, whenever, just next time, don't wait too long to collab, I respect your pen.

A Bond

He came up to me angrier than I've ever seen him. When he approached me, I could see blood in his eyes. Ayo, Inf, I'm gonna body this nikka, this is the second time he disrespected my gangster, there's not going to be a third, he asked for a problem . . . I'm the answer. I could tell he was way beyond the point of no-return. He's sweating profusely, pacing back and forth, mumbling between grinds of teeth. He put on gloves, took out a box and started loading clips. Fall back! You're ready to act on anger, give me the gat, let's plan, give it at least one night then we'll touch 'em when the drama simmers.

Na, I'm going to make an example out of him tonight, I can't let you do that, you have too much to lose. Lose? If I don't react, my respect will be lost. Is earning respect greater than the love for your fam? You're ready to give that all up for one man? Let's pull up tomorrow and clear the air, I'll freeze his team up and make him fight you fair. I would love that but what's gonna happen the next time when we bump heads and you're not there? You can't protect me forever, besides he threatened me, he said the next time he sees me, my life is over. Okay, this is what we're going to do, we're going to drive by in my car, it's tinted they won't know it's you, I'll drive slow, you point him out and his crew. I need to know who we're going against. He agreed.

That's him right there. That's his boys too. Copy. I got you. We'll deal with this in the morning. Go, get some sleep . . . early the next morning . . . Breaking News . . . a New York man was arrested for a deadly shooting spree in the Bronx, four dead and a couple of bystanders injured, police shot the perp but he is expected to live . . . Baby, baby, wake up, look, what mom, leave me alone, I'm tired, baby, please look . . . it's your father . . . The man had this to say to reporters when

Albert 'Infinite the Poet' Carrasco

asked why did he do it while being whisked away . . . I couldn't let those men become the reason why I no longer have a son . . . What happened, baby?

Baptism

My wisdom works like baptism, I'm blessings heads. Infinite's urban water crosses borders like abyss when I surf airwaves. I'm internationally known cause of my wordplay, ayo he's cray, mo that dude is lit, that's depending on where I'm at, some lack ebonics so I hear "Namaste" after I spit. Harsh life poetry, real life spoken word, nonfiction verses on oppressions that curse us.

My forte is manipulating letters to paint pictures of the beginning and returning ash when dealing with boy or girl bathing in that Pyrex glass . . . the end-result when hunger, greed and the street clash. I'll cause a negative ripple effect by glorifying any time of my past other than stating that the past is what made me who I am.

You can't tell people that are willing to sacrifice life to gain by any means necessary that you've been here and there and did this and that from owning traps and pushn grams . . . That'll be the door opener, "if he did it, I can do it, me and him are the same", what I do say clearly is . . . I've been here and there, had this and that and would give it all back just not to be a sole survivor . . . Nobody wants to feel that type of pain, how I win is by shedding light on the darkness in the game.

Raids, kites, last rights, daily mourning, twenty-four-hour reminiscing of those that are missing . . .

I constantly wonder how life could've been if most of the men I ran with didn't relocate to prison and heaven. Everyone would have a book ghost-written, instead of just being a band of brothers dealing with drugs and guns, we all would be authors on life in the slums.

Got Fat

I got fat gettn the white girl off, dudes tried to get chicken but it ain't happen, I call 'em Kate moss. My work spoke for itself; I didn't even have to Polly. I just kicked my feet up and became a boss.

Poverty had me greedy, I reed, chefd and tossed, wasn't lookn for pitchers I flipped my own money, OG's used to say you're seven thirty, lil' homie, I'll be like na, I'm just guaranteeing a meal for the family, I promised that we'll never go hungry, until I level up, I'll be Dolo by the bitty or in that nycha lobby filthy.

It was that time, I needed a staff for the lines, put on dudes I knew since 138 and went wild on ps8, we'll be sauced scheming on jake, wait for it . . . Aight they jumped out . . . skate, go up, change clothes then back to handing out packs behind the red door and counting cake.

Back to celo and pitching quarters constantly getting interrupted by dudes holding straws and quarter waters, can I get credit, can I get a short, everybody is looking for that color that's famous in the hood like newport, it was one hell of a ride till best friends started to become victims of homicide . . . the game became a blood sport.

One got laid out . . . We rode, the second got laid out . . . We rode, third, fourth, fifth we rode, etcetera, etcetera till the "we" was no longer . . . Just like it started, I was solo on the road trying to plan a future while praying to my deceased friends . . . Please help me my brothers, don't let me become a statistic of murder.

I must've made them work overtime, sorry fam, I know you guys are now relaxed, I retired before I expired so I'm giving back by showing the facade's reality through urban syntax.

Shine

Watch me shine, I'm lyrically in my prime, it's the i n f one of the realest urban griots of our time. since day one I've been a threat, I'm still mastering the wordplay craft by using the twelve dropped letters from the alphabet. I'm a dark life scriber, fast life reciter, if I had a chariot it would've been sluggish because of all the bodies of my homies that got scorched in the fire. My blood ruined sheets on gurneys, my life and freedom constantly were in the hands of trial attorneys, I was into polygamy, married the white girl, blue steel and red streets . . . it was unholy matrimony, I had lust for them cause they gave me money, protection and blocks to invest in. My childhood and my young teen years went by celebrating the emancipation from poverty with my hustling peers, by twenty, I'm mourning two, by thirty almost the entire crew, that dirty money wasn't appealing like it used to. I was no longer dependent but by that time my rap sheet doubled the length of my deceased codefendants. I had to reinvent myself and flip from a narcotic acrobat to leaving traces of ink on white lines, I manufacture heroin, coke and crack when I rhyme, the authorities phone tap me just to hear me spit it recklessly, I hear applause after about three minutes and twenty, I am what the dapper tried to be . . . untouchable with street poetry, I don't have to worry about my sons inheriting my drama like Jr Gotti.

We've Made It

Poverty is a thing of the past, life was a cold, cold world, we wondered how long it would last. The forecast changed, things got in order, lives were rearranged as money got longer. We moved out the jects to try to avoid tradition and make a generation gap, ya know to raise children that don't think the only way to make money is owning traps, till this day we suffer the consequences of trial and era to make life better for others . . . We just weren't going to look back. Every day was an advance, yesterday wouldn't get a glance cause all we'll see are bodies with blatant causes of death, no need for autopsies, we know slugs killed them, no need for human dissection. We spent years in lobbies or sitting on benches in housing tenements dealing with natures elements for dead presidents. We went back-to-back to burials, each time it was back to Moving packs in front of the latest makeshift mural, we had dreams, we dreamt of capital and how to possess it by any means, unfortunately for us it was through weight on beams. We don't hide the life, we explain it in detail, good times ended with murder or jail, life spans got shorter, our souls weren't for sale, we just lived life a certain way feeling like the world had our worth less than retail. When opportunity came, we left the block, we kept the hustler mentality and became business men, they're doing them and I'm pushing myself like cooked rock, a poetic author of hard knocks . . . We made it, we became tone deaf when the fat lady sung and hell serenaded.

Albert 'Infinite the Poet' Carrasco

Born-Day

You can go harder than you'll ever go and your hardest won't be harder than my everyday poetic urban flow. I'm a child that was born in the belly of the beast, the ghetto was my amnio, the jects were my umbilical, cocaine was the placenta surrounding me as I stretched out of fetal in a nycha lobby, the concrete jungle and the hustle gave birth to a newborn baby. The government is Albert, the attribute is infinite and my last name is CHP, the hood claimed me, my born-to-die mother and father are Castle Hill and Randall, I couldn't get 'em to move, they're stationary, so I had no choice but to grow up in their vicinity. Since I couldn't suck on momma's titty for leche the revolution started like a young che, ayo put me on, I'll give you yours before I finished the bomb . . . I was on. I was knowledge wisdom . . . an understanding, a lil' dude learning the ropes of Coke and dope to cope in housing. When I was born there was others born along side of me, a boom of doomed babies, ya know brother and sister statistics of prison and murder, we rode till many got life or died, after sentences and homicides the pedal was still to the metal I had to ride, trials and burials were the outcome for putting in hustler miles on the expressway to prison and genocide.

Inferno

I heard the wind howling, and I felt its cold, that's with my windows closed, so I slept with my clothes, had the same blanket since 5 years old, it was short, so I had an option, whether to cover my chest or my frozen toes, it was too short to cover both.

Fire

I loved him so, he was about six feet, crowns around certain teeth, golden brown, waves circling 360, the bread winner of the carrasco family, he was my daddy, honorably discharged from the military, while skipping rocks in wisdom at just twelve, mamma told me we lost him.

Flame

Welfare, face to face, fighting evictions cases at two fifty broadway, that's how moms started her days off, dad died and moms got laid off, surplus food in cabinets depleted, refrigerator is on, but there's nothing in it to keep cold, or nothing to take out to be heated, the freezer is one huge mess of ugly ice, I didn't like this life!

Hell

Jumbos jumbos, red top blue top, from being hungry I found a way to eat, treys nicks dimes, no shorts, cop and go, no lines! I wasn't happy, I just wore an evil grin, just as evil as grin, I knew this wasn't me, I was taken over by jinn. From a cold room to a cold world, I became the streets' next of kin, pain suffering death incarceration, this is what the street plays, ghetto music on heavy rotation.

Albert 'Infinite the Poet' Carrasco

Super Nova

I now walk the path of Allah with Jesus guiding me, an anomaly, before dad died, he filled the book of life in my third eye, the highest degrees, a d moms taught me christianity. My views are different from how the average man sees, I would be called a philosopher by Aristotle, Plato and Socrates, I have wisdom like the seven seas, I spit wisdom to enlighten the seven's seeds.

I dealt with the fire and lived through the flames walked through hell, now it's all over, Infinite the poet, sideways 8 my trademarked lemniscate, burning in super nova.

Construction / Demolition

I paved a path that's called the strip, the ave, the trap, the block, I helped with the construction of roads leading to drug dens for the purchase of rock, I tried to construct an empire like the state building brick by brick with my poor neighbors, trying to profit off the addicted and the sick coke and dope abusers. Inf got the schematics, the blueprint, the measurements, 10 into every 30, the mathematics for the substance that changes from a powder to a solid, dried it, then bagged it in tiny vials or miniature zip lock plastics. Played in that other arena with my manitos, mask, gloves, grinders and manito, spoon and needles, scotch taped glassines, ten to a bundle, and stamps to label the lethal, took orders in a hole in the wall. I did it all. Fast chicks fast wips, sports cars or 4x4's, glocks, sigs, reugers, desert e 44's, bullet proofs fitted behind door panels, ready for war, driving through the nitty gritty city trying to avoid hostile juveniles from getting lucky shots off at me, I ate lights to prevent my forehead from horn beeping, on point never sleeping . . .

I paved a path that's called the strip, the ave, the trap, the block, I helped with the construction of roads leading to drug dens for the purchase of rock. Now I'm back to those roads to do demolition with my pen, I'm sticking it in the pavement to lift the blood-stained cement. I'm back to the block, I'm standing on corners reciting like those solo preachers you see in the hood with a mic amp and speakers, I'm ready to knock on doors like Jehovah's because I witnessed so many deaths, so I'm trying to save my sisters and brothers from becoming next. I was puppeteered and so was my peers; I cut my strings. My people would've too but they're no longer here. They're in the Feds, maxi max facilities or monuments in cemeteries since the eighties or nineties. The streets are venomous. I heard so many tell me how they gonna make it, I told them it's not gonna happen. That's a promise, you know what was the outcome? I just gave them a moment of silence.

My Ensemble

Shoulder strap gats, timbs, fatigues, champion hoodie, darkies a vest and a pocket full of soft and hard blow was my everyday ensemble, the sets bellaco the title is capo, I spit the ying and yang of blood Capitol, the ups and downs of dug and perico, the pros and cons of material. You can get so much money that it'll get you angry to manually count, you can spend without tallying the amount, you can fly overseas without luggage cause wherever the destination is the first thing you do is go on shopping sprees, women . . . they'll come in herds, power and respect is gained when the streets hear you're letting things fly and moving birds, Toyota Nissan and Honda turn to Mercedes Audi and beemers as that money gets longer, wants become a thing of the past, the struggle is over. That's the outcome for 1% . . . what most likely is going to happen to the other 99% is they're going to become felon repeaters, old cell visitors, rags to riches, rags to riches wave riders until it crashes ashore and they can't come up anymore. Shopping spree money goes to lawyers when caught by dees, the women . . . they'll bounce like middle finger up, boy please, power and respect ends with the end of your endz . . . Ayo, he's washed up mo, that'll be the slick shit coming out of mouths of "good time" only so-called friends, those leased German vehicles are repossessed because you can't pay for the rest, that's what happens to the lucky ones, the unlucky bid forever or take their last breath when slugs go in mouths, ears, heads and chest.

Everyday Life

I'll come out first, search the roof, stairs and lobby before skeeyuuu'n for safety, five minutes later I'm flanked by a dirty army, concrete seals bunkered in New York City housing authority, Bosses, pitchers, back door and park side watchers, ghost spotters, steerers, loud rollers, cello players, band stuffers from pitchn quarters and of course shot callers.

We never denied short money on the block, if they had four for a nick, we'd open the slab and chip off one fifth from that rock, didn't take change tho because pockets filled with e plurubis rattles when blow'n it from bajando, they'll turn off their radio and listen to the Ching Ching Ching and be like there they go, we needed to see a dead prez face for that before and after . . . Powder or bass . . . We can't do menudo, yeah, I'm Spanish, the name is bellaco, I stood silent, but my gats holla . . . dee me lo.

Coke spots moved liked doped blocks, blow had that her-ron flow, fiends would've out number tenants if we didn't enforce cop and go. We were poor and tired of settling for less, setting it off isn't something I'll suggest, you'll be brainless coming at us or making our money regress. I can't build with dudes from the sandbox, they're dead or always in the box, a result from real life hard knocks, bars and last hallmarks, relieving the past I see muzzles flash and the looks on kinfolk when they passed, or that guilty verdict shock laugh, that's me now and then reminiscing on the ave, blood bath after blood bath, funeral after funeral I stood chasing red cash, the hardest thing in the world was walking away from it all and looking at the aftermath . . . trails of phlebotomy, new corpse over old bodies, I hear yells and screams when words aren't even uttered, that's my mind putting sound to vision when I'm thinking about fam that was murdered.

I see my peeps pacing back and forth in cells like there's something to do and they're going to be late, I see them tallying days when they don't have release dates, the average man wouldn't want to see what I see and feel what I feel but I hone in on it to write pain expressing hurt from ugly fate, it's infinite the poet, the lemniscate and I rep Mitchell llama the projects and section eight, I was trapped in the trap, I'm here to open that gate. We can get paper, let's ride, we can get paper without urban genocide, you can even keep your street team . . . If you listen to me talk about my team's jail time and homicides.

Yeah, we all can get rich in the street, I can open up and make a million a year, in that time I'll lose about four to tradition, two hundred fifty thousand isn't worth losing my surviving peers, we're supposed to burry our parents, in the game that's not apparent, by twenty-one most birthday boys are absent, moms and dads either celebrate or mourn life after death, then wonder who's going to be there when they take their last breath and who's going to be there to lay them to rest.

Albert 'Infinite the Poet' Carrasco

About That Life

We kept the kitchen shades down all year round, we kept clips with vest eating rounds, we kept multiple connections just in case the other isn't around and retainers for when them doors got kicked down. Every day was about the hustle, we broke night after night tryn to bubble two for a nickel long Taj Mahaj's lookn like religious temples, stomping comp was quite simple.

My numbers were lower, my grade was higher and the fact we were smarter and hungrier made them give up . . . it was a no-brainer. We walked out nycha lobbies with arms open shoutn the world is ours . . . That was the daily state of mind of youngens earning five figures each shift on the grind. Foreign whips, quads, bikes and exotic women brought character to the bricks, we wore so much jewels and gems CHP looked like a slum diamond district.

That's what life was like for us for years, I'm looking at the "we made it face" glow on my peers, wants are a thing of the past, we used to think about the days when we asked our mothers for a dollar and they would get screw-faced and say "from where, my chocha" then burst out in laughter . . . we don't have to ask them anymore, times changed now we give them dead prez showers.

The reactions to actions have yet to emerge, every day we woke up was a good day to splurge, a new Cuban, a new wardrobe, when the blacksmith came sell'n gats we bought that that that, instead of letting the enemy get a chance to get strapped we bought the entire duffle bag, literally he didn't even get that back, we bought new rims with sticky low pros for shine and grip as we bx to harlem no brake bat. Our destination was cambo or Branson before ordering willie burgers and Half-and-halfs to munch as big boy toys took ave baths.

Life was lovely but it got ugly quickly, now we have to keep the kitchen shades down to prevent observations, we kept vest eating rounds to prevent more assassinations . . . It isn't pretty watchn a teammate bleed out, sprawled out on the ground. We had to keep multiple connections; so, when we were hot, we could eat somewhere else while on the run.

Scorned Consequences

My son is a good boy. He would've never hurt no one that didn't want to hurt him. No, he wasn't a saint but neither was the others. They all lived the same lives. As mothers of hustlers, we pray for the best but expect the worst. The actions that occurred took a child away from all of us, we all feel the repercussion to their decisions. It could've easily been me here speaking to a defendant before sentencing hoping to get my son's killer to become a lifer and you on the other side pleading for mercy for junior. No matter which way you look at it, it's a lose-lose situation. So, the ugly picture you're painting of my son here in court for murder is two-faced. The only reason my child is alive is because he shot first when his life was threatened, as we all know because of the evidence and witnesses on the stand, your son was found with a gun in his hand . . . Get her out of here before I charge her with contempt . . . No, your honor . . . she's right, I want her son to pay for his crime . . . but I do want him to see daylight . . . Thank you! it's true, I hate to say it but we both knew, there's no need to infinitely lose two. They hug in tears as the judge sentenced him to the lesser charge of twenty-five years.

Healthy in Heaven

I think 'bout my team that didn't make it when I'm spittn,
when I'm finished the booth or a stage becomes a hospice for mics . . .
I leave 'em in grave condition.
I see blood and death while mentally reliving homicides.
I smell embalming fluid and formaldehyde from a victim of cocaine genocide.
I hear yells and screams from people
standn next to a ditch . . .
When that body goes inside,
when lash touches lash for a prolonged period of time,
murder scenes cross my mind.
As I lay my head to rest at night,
I see men that died in hell . . .
Healthy in heaven

Albert 'Infinite the Poet' Carrasco

A Poet Since 1984

Since 1984, I've been a poet. I just didn't know it, the streets were teaching me urban life apostrophe while I was running around dirty, no hygiene, I'm talking about the burner at my waistline, blood money and boy and girl packs in my jeans. I was trying to turn poverty to wealthy by making dreams reality, I was living poetry.

WIC, food stamps, face to face, monthly struggles to eat and to keep our place, the peeking thru closed shades, wars and raids for arms, fish scale, A grade and all the money I made, death of my father, homicide crime scenes from men that were as close as brothers, those same type of brothers got cuffed in the nineties, brought down to bury their mother, then father, missed the birth of their children and grandchildren because it's sixteen years into the two gees and they're still bidding.

The flash, the sound, the ground, blood loss, operating, pain, fighting to conscious regain . . . I learnt the reactions from someone having slugs with my name. Financial freedom, twenty-four-hour splurging, blowing stacks on liquor, jewels, clothes, bikes, whips, trips, black, brown and green crushed into leaf, licked and burned till it had an orange tip and till it burnt finger tips then put in ashtrays with Hawaiian Punch clips.

The high life . . . materialism, luxury, euphoria took hits . . . hit rock bottom and did it all over, rock bottom, rich, rock bottom, rich, got addicted to lie because of type of roller coaster. Many expired, I lost too many members of the team learning the blueprint on how to prevent our teens and young men from trying to reign supreme with digitals and triple beams because they're poor and want to live the so-called American Dream.

Guidance

My footsteps are guided and followed by shadows, entities, angels, I am just a vessel. Growing up without my father, I suffered . . . I didn't understand that he became my watcher, my first and ultimate protector, every death after made me stronger . . . but at the time I felt it made me weaker.

I would scream out to the heavens . . . take me with you! Why should I remain on hell's surface? I wouldn't hear a response, but they answered . . . they kept me alive to fulfill our purpose.

They got serenaded by the pale moon dancer and introduced to the reaper . . . then became my keeper. I made them work overtime to prevent the end of my lifeline, my demise could've happened many times. I know it was my dad that stopped that slug from hitting my lung and killing his son because I saw him . . . in my heart, I know it's my homies that helped me evade street-life fatalities in the slums.

The combination of deceased family and friends made me a poetician, that's a poet and a mortician, my pieces are urban benediction, blessing before crucifixion of every mother's immaculate conception, instead of nails on hands and feet, its nails to seal a coffin.

I got tired of saying bye to my men, the last to die was Abdul Ghaffar Abdul from SOMX and we buried him by hand.

I know what family and friends go through at the time of death, I went through it over and over, I saw the tears along with crying out loud, at times I would close my eyes, so I didn't see the released doves flying towards the clouds, but that didn't stop me from hearing the pain because there was no way to temporarily go deaf. My duty is to teach positivity from experienced negativity. I was saved to save.

You can't preach to those whose prayers went unanswered, they're angered, so I teach because my young kin is becoming endangered, they're exploited to what's imported, they get addicted to money then become a docket number or a statistic of murder. I don't have a choice but the youth does . . . they can sit back and ask themselves do they want their friends and family around them in the physical or would they rather have them around in the form of angels?

When people return to the essence, we beg for a last time to see and feel their presence, I still do know that, that opportunity is past tense. I appreciate my guardians, don't get me wrong, I just dreamt of us growing old and rich together . . . I guess I slept too long.

Money

I lived life hearing a repetitive tick tick ticking, the sound of time quickly passing cause I was speeding. when it came to chasing dough inf was on turbo constantly cheffn what peeps was smoking adding to the deterioration of our ozone, went to owning blocks soon after playing with hasbro, went to jail at fifteen years old because of the protection I carried while making sales.

Every action was high stakes, there was a chance your body will die and your soul escapes, or a chance of a bus ride chain ganged up state, if lucky them deals will go well and I could continue to eat well while residue staining mommas' plates. I risked my freedom daily, was prone to violence regardless of consequence, if you look at my rap sheet, it'll read guns drugs guns drugs in that sequence.

I was lost climbing ranks to be boss, I was determined to get there no matter the cost, when I got knocked, I paid bail or bond, came out and continued on to become the don. I lived expendable for street credentials cause in that field it's detrimental.

My mind was on survival mode, the fire in my eye had me cross the devil's threshold, I was like a parolee, the hot streets had a dollar hold on me, I was blind-eyed, couldn't see, all I saw was visions of owning a monopoly, with dreams of growing into a dynasty, but the dudes I rolled with died so nasty, like just space where brains used to be, like covers covering bodies and sheets over splattered anatomy, like a mother cradling her slow reaching and slow breathing son yelling somebody call nine-one-one.

I was lied to, my goal is to enlighten youths, so they have an option before going through pusher adoption, before they face ninety-nine problems, that white girl will be the reason for all of them, more money more drama, the thicker the body armor, more time delivered by your honor. I didn't come to glorify the hustle, I'm here to bust bubbles, everything thing that glitters ain't gold, you see the bling, the fancy car driving, the 1000-dollar daily ensemble, those are the ones to yet witness how this world is so cold, they haven't touched enough homies that felt so cold, so they're still trying to reach their street dreaming goal.

The game never changes, just the players, if I take all the dead and stockpile them, to get to the top, you'll need to place scaffolding, and one of those manual elevators.

My Scroll

My mind holds a never-ending poetic scroll, hear ye hear ye. I see words scattering in my head written in calligraphy, I'm like the ghetto pied piper, the mic is my flute, I travel city to city speaking urban truth to urban youth, I'm in the hood like the church of ladder day, I'm the urban spoken protégé.

I lived what I speak, I'm the one that got the finger pointed at like "there's the bad guy" when I walked the streets, wasn't bad at all, my situation was called being poor, I just did bad things to earn money as soon as I stepped out my project housing door.

I been through wars, thirty years of tours deadly attacks like in Iraq or Darfur, but from genocide, from our own neighbors' next door. I've been around since Ronald Reagan let gigantic ships like the titanic doc in our region, it was politics, bricks upon bricks of cocaine with the recipe to cook to an oily goo, it was quickly consumed and abused, it made money but the pushers and sellers didn't really know what chaos would come from the aftermath . . . murder, prostitution, robberies, trials for class a felony, reco acts for just a few cracks, = confined for an eternity.

I strongly write and recite this urban reality, especially when I pause and stare at the bullet holes in my body, or when I look at the funeral cards from everybody, or when I look at my oldest son, he's 11, I was twelve pushing caps in lobbies. My third eye blinks ink, so you can see what I saw, what the street life has in store, before that tap on your door from the reaper's sword.

Infinite Teachings

They should replace lie-braries with infinite scriptoriums. Schools should have my poems being read to entire grades in auditoriums, wardens should put me on payrolls m inmates can have a better chance of staying home after they max out or get paroled with my verbal rehabilitation. Sky writers should fly around leaving smoke trails that form into urban stanzas written by me to be read by the underground population and the "next up" generation. New York City trains, busses and taxis should be advertising my "each one teach one" apostrophe. There should be karaoke machines in every ghetto, so people can help me spread my words like Muslim lessons and the gospel. I'm no narcissist, but I lived in the fire, so I speak about hell on earth better, I forecast fate like a fortune-teller.

I Thank God for My Hood

The slums of the Bronx are like a giant vagina, I was born and raised in the hood . . . My middle name should've been NYCHA. Skyscraper projects . . . The color of blood, apartments filled with boxes and storage bins sitting on cracked tiles like there was a flood, arroz y betuelas, rice and peas, ox tail and beef stew, boriquas gettn their soul food on and morenos cooking abuelitas recipe for that Spanish herb accented stew, it's a mixed community . . . that's how we do. Poverty was something more than most had in common, the Apple was rotten, we had to hustle, gains were ill-gotten. I wouldn't be the poet I am, if I didn't get dealt the cards that the illuminati handed out to society. They gave me joy . . . then pain. They gave me sunshine . . . then rain, in order to learn one, I had to learn the other to be a nonfiction hood life author. I lived in hell like I was one of god's forgotten sons, was too much for the devil to handle, so I got labeled a rebel of satan. My kin and I tried to bread win in hous'n, we wanted to live like businessmen, so we became them, stocks and bonds, na, employment was stackn paper by pushing bombs of cooked Coke and bundles of heroin. We become young men of business, hoping the hoods cracked tar and unevenly laid concrete would lead us to the road to the riches, I can't lie, it did, along with time and eternal bids, jail and six-feet ditches . . . there would've been less ditches if brains could get stitches. In the hood, I learnt reactions to actions, so I use my voice and pen to paint pictures of reenactment to move the stagnant. Here I am today, AL carrasco, infinite the poet, a product of my environment, a survivor of the evil card dealer, went from asking for credit at the bodega, to touching keys like a piano player, to feeling like I'm top of the world, to that cold feeling that takes over when I go to cemeteries and visit those buried under it, to a writer known from the hood to different hoods in different continents, I never in a million years would've that would become me while sitting on my sofa in 6m looking out my project window thinking, what would become of me? As my waistline held the gun, while my pockets held what needed to be changed into currency, I rep my hood hard body.

Albert 'Infinite the Poet' Carrasco

Shows

Every time the poet did a show, there he was, the old man in the back that always gets emotional when the poet blows. He's a huge fan. He comes in when the poets on stage and he leaves before he gets off so they never got a chance to have a formal introduction.

It seems like this old man understands the poet's harsh reality poetry. When the poet recites about drugs, guns and murder, the old man cries; when he recites about surviving those times, the old man cheers; when he recites about overcoming the addiction, to addiction he stands at attention with his curved spine and gives the poet a standing ovation.

One day, the poet tricked him, he told the host to introduce him but he stood in the crowd waiting for the old man to enter . . . and like click work he did, the poet said . . . sir, I want to thank you for always coming to see me . . . up close, he looks more elderly. He says, Mr. poet, I've known you since you were kid, it makes me so happy to see you're still here and not dead or doing a lifelong bid.

The hairs on my body rise when you story-tell because I know what you're talking about quite well, just like you, I've lost many people dealing with cocaine, I feel your pain, I'm so happy you made it out, not a lot of people are alive like you and me. The poet is amazed that the old fragile-looking man knows him, he says why do you stand in the hall till I get on stage and leave before we can shake hands upon introduction?

The old man says because I'm the start of everything you went through and I'm so sorry, it's me . . . your first coke connection. The poet hugs him . . . no worries, we all did what needed to be done to survive. There's no animosity. He's no longer just the old man, no need for anonymity, he's a living legend from trap life history.

Word Player

Inf is a true word playa, don't need to say mic check before going in cause if the mic ain't workn, I'm still going in acapella, I'm a spoken word artist, a street corner lyricist, I break down the game of Caine like a gem star in the hand of an igneous chemist. In this genre, ain't nobody doing it better, I got that butta like when I was advertising my color, I hate when peeps say Inf you're in my top five, I be like, yeah, get the other four for a lyrical war, I bet they won't survive, they won't even show up cause they know I'm really from streets and spit facts while they Mac and- make up- lies.

Everybody is hard, everybody got weight, everybody bust choppers, everybody is a killer, everybody sounds the same with that weak shit, they sideline glorify the life of traffic, infinites a hustler's son, hustln in the slums was in my genetics, bosses was my demographic, my name buzzes like quads, kx's and cr's in the projects, full-blown, where I'm from there's not many bori's that made it to the throne, we had the hood lookn like vintage la perla, so we could feel like we're home, gettn gwap gettn dome, if we wanted a new spizzy to expand . . . a trap got overthrown.

This is where the realness comes in and y'all separate me from the phony . . . For the love of money, I lost a lot of my homies, bloodshed painted the town red like cool g said, life sentences got some living dead, funerals and trials took a lot of bread, mothers of deceased friends hold me and say they love me, but cry cause they remember junior before the hole in his head, fathers strapped up for revenge, we had to tell the senior polity, we know you're angry because of the death of your son, but your wife needs you more than ever, you have to sit out this one, children ask me "how was my daddy", talking about them in the past isn't fun, drugs guns, kites, last rights, I'm an urban problem when I spit or write.

Armageddon

Poverty led to crime, crime led to wealth, jail and a lot of flatlines, the lucky ones got send up and came home, stashed something for later usage, sport knife wounds or bullet holes and evaded the process of getting picked up off dirty New York streets like garbage. Empty pockets, dockets, because of narcotics grave sites border traps in projects, the cross brizzy takes me pass the dome-less home of my street family in sin city, the east Bronx, the nitty gritty . . . Saint Raymond's holds the leaves that fell from the tree. Intricate plans, table grinding and Pyrex pots, manito, soda, bundles, slabbed rocks, Mariaaaaa . . . We spotted them cops, subiendo, bajando, they're coming up or down the block, spottas spotted hadda as soon as they entered nycha and watched where the ghost was dropped. Bellaco, manteca, perico . . . Soft and duro, no comp when competing against puro. War . . . shells drop, eyes blown out, knock knock, there's a new peephole on doors, blood on walls and floors, lights out on the first tour for first four, blood-thirsty to make a million off raw. Who I be, Infinite, the knowledge and wis wiz, square . . . Biz, high grain for any test or pop quiz? Settn it off . . . I don't suggest it, kin-folk will have something go from front thru back regardless if ya vested, I'm positive, so unless it's forced, things won't blow, green lights can be given but I'd rather idle on yellow to avoid red puddles. I didn't choose poetry, poetry chose me, living in the bricks and going to lots and lots of viewings to listen to eulogies gave me concrete imagery, I am living urban apostrophe, this is not Plato, Aristotle and Socrates philosophies, these are words manifested through witnessed tragedies that led to Armageddon for many men.

Chosen

I've been chosen to use spoken to enlighten, after the life I lived I don't question . . . why me? I know why. I was tortured, the streets forced me to watch day one homies motionless after being murdered, I suffered, using blow to change poverty to wealthy, I continued to do so, luck must've been on my side when slugs ripped through my torso, one minute I'm looking at my deceased dad, the next I'm back on the block with cast and cane, vest, gat and packs of hard cocaine, I took one for the team, it's all part of the game.

It's business as usual just with my mind full of t h c and my body full of Tylenol with codeine as I feed fiends, ain't no bitch in me, I had something to prove, as long as I was breathing, I won't lose. Well, that's what I thought, I lost more than what I ever gained dealing with import on hot blocks of New York. How much is a soul? To me, it's worth more than what was ever sold, what's so cold is that there's no turning back when you're dressed in dark blue or black, with eyes and lips glued in a hearse taking that final lap, many times I followed that last lap, buried them, then again . . . right back to the trap.

The last death would be the last death is something I kept saying, but nine one ones kept coming in because of more slayings, I was on the road to the riches and wasn't straying, it got to a point where new doves flew before the last member of the crew started decaying. Everybody expired, I retired without breaking up my white girl marriage, laid low then reemerged on the scene to generation salvage.

No Longer Here

Coming up with men that are no longer here is hard, during good and bad times I think about those thinking about me in the yard and those that went back to God. I'm one of the strongest but knowing I can't hand back freedom or resuscitate my brothers in thug mansion makes me feel powerless. At times, I want to gather up the squad, strap up, jack some armored vehicles, place c4 on prison walls, then drive in with the convoy after detonation and release all my allies who already have over two decades of so-called rehabilitation. Since I can't resuscitate, I wish I had the power of life rejuvenation, like if I die today, I'll come back to life tomorrow . . . that way I won't be full of sorrow because every once in a while, I'll commit suicide and spend the day with those that met early fates and passed the pearly gates because of homicides. I've taken too many losses, been to blown trials, buried partners, managers and pitchers from adults to juveniles, we didn't take a lot of flicks so for a few of them funeral cards are my only pics. I hate reminiscing with new cats, I be like, yo, y'all remember . . . na, they don't because none of them guys were there and that's when it triggers memories and it hits hard because the guys that would know what I'm talking about are no longer here. We had blasphemous poor kid syndrome; I have love for the new generation but it kills me how my era of good fellas went through extinction. Drugs, guns, drama, wars, us forgotten suns arose and fell like solstices in the slums, possession of materialism and shoe box prezy's continued to be our goal, let's show the incarcerated and the deceased that we can make it . . . that led to more roof top taps, soldiers in caskets and a motorcade following a hearse showing the hood where we're circling how we roll. I would do anything to relive life with friends of mine . . . I often catch myself turning back the clock as if I can rewind time.

Questions

Where I'm from, I always wondered where would I go? Would I ever get to leave the ghetto? Would I ever move from my apartment into a house to rake leaves in summer and shovel snow in the winter? Would I have a two-car garage? Instead of walking a few steps to my shared incinerator, would I ever get an opportunity to take a long walk on my property to throw away garbage? Would I be able to turn up a thermostat instead of tapping on steam pipes so housing could turn up heat? Would I ever have my own pool so me and my hood friends can swim in instead of scratching cans on concrete to open both ends then aim hydrant water at each other to keep cool? Would I ever live the American dream? Those were the thoughts I had before street adoption, before I used scales to weigh options, before settling for less and continuing living the poor life . . . poverty adaptation. I wanted equality, I wanted to live like people outside NYCHA property. I had ambition, that plus wishful thinking put me in all type of unwanted conditions, hell's come sutra, awkward positions . . . like me in prison, like me on a gurney bleeding, like me looking at a body and positively identifying a homie through glass partitions, or like me pulling a plug after everybody kisses them. The good that comes from the game gets overshadowed by the pain of those ill-gotten gains. Survivors shine bright but mourn morning, noon and night, but paying car note, paying rent, purchasing clothes, jewels and other materialistic items from profit made with dead men doesn't feel right. It's been years since I retired and I still see doctors' faces and hear their voices telling me my man expired. It's hard to enjoy yourself, laugh and have fun after Armageddon, it's hard to rest at peace when there's so many that forever rest in peace in paradise amongst the heavens. Reactions to actions of the past still linger, it's like having an invisible thread of yesterday around my finger so I can always remember. My pursuit of happiness by using a Pyrex to earn riches ended with anguish. Poverty scared me, I had no fear in dying to obtain currency, I wanted bags of dirty money as heavy as bags of dirty laundry, I wanted to sip on momo and abso instead of Malta and coco rico, just like my friends, I wanted to better my family, not watch homies move out the projects into a cemetery. We wanted to excel not regress and look at a pale mother in a new black dress . . . cause of death . . . perico cut with the ghetto.

A Father-and-Son Story

I raised him to be a better man than I was. I taught him manners and respect, I taught him how to make his dreams, goals and to pursue them until they're achieved. No matter how many obstacles, trials and tribulations he may face, in himself he must always believe. He listened and learnt, he's on the right path.

I'm a proud father, my boy is my pride and joy. In elementary, he was a fast learner; in intermediate, he was the poster child; in high school, he was the bar, the one teachers used as an example to others not up to par. After he graduated, he went back to school . . . but it wasn't college. Everything changed.

We quarreled all day, argued all night, I swear if I didn't love him so much, many of those heated exchanges would've ended with a fist fight. My past is giving him a green light, a pass to own blocks . . . his new school is hard knocks.

He met up with other ex-hustlers' sons, they put the plug in him after everything I taught him. Junior, don't you know, you have power because of your father? He's respected, we can run wild, we'll be protected. We could make thousands of dollars, why waste four more years of your life being a scholar? Fu.. a job! You can be a boss and run an empire.

He fell to temptation, he didn't understand that he didn't need them, they needed him and that was just because they needed him in order to get material from my old connections. I tried to explain to my son that I didn't enjoy the life and that I got caught up because of poverty, I showed him my bullet scars, my friends' funeral cards, I showed him the kites I've been receiving from dudes behind bars since the eighties to the two g's, he's been with me to cemeteries, watching me bow my head and pray to the ole g's, I told him, that I made that connection millions and they never helped with retainers, bail, bond or for burials of those ole g's when they were children.

I explained to him that I left the game to raise him, to have my last name multiplied by him, not for him to try to make my old life a tradition. He still wasn't listening; we're going back and forth. I said, okay, okay, I'll be right back. I went to a neighbor to get a gat and a vest; I went back home put on my fatigues and hoody and told him lets go, I'm ready.

He's looking at me as if I'm playing, I told him I'll sell the drugs, I'll shoot the guns, I'll go to jail and die for you, all you have to do is stand there and soak it all in for experience and urban education . . . come on! What's the decision gonna be, junior? He realizes, I'm being real . . . he jumps on me and hugs me tightly, he says . . . take off that vest and give back the gun, I'm not going to lose my father . . . I hug him tighter and say . . . I'm not going to lose my son!

Ahead of My Time ... from the Streets to the Stages

The Way I Grew Up

I grew up drinking ponche made with Malta and eating pan con huevo frito and oxtail soup that was tradition in my great grandmother's and grandmother's kitchen on weekends. I knew those were meals I could depend on, the other five days for the first two weeks of the month there was rice with corned beef, rice with eggs, Mac & cheese with mashed potatoes and corn on rotation, the last two weeks we had to make uninvited dinner visitations or deal with temporary starvation.

I thought that was life, I was young, I didn't understand oppression. Before I became infinite from bellaco doing a three-decade street bid, I was innocent Albertito, the naive kid. Poverty + 1984 corrupted me, the birth of cook Coke made me a crack baby. Great grandma returned to the essence. In 84, I was twelve, that's the age where I last saw my dad's presence and grandma moved to the sunshine state, so now it's even harder to put food on plates.

Hitting rock bottom created infinite da problem, somebody gave me a pack and I didn't even have a trap, I made one, I learnt how to melt grams in jars of jam then went from trapless to traffic jams in the slum. I was happy that there was surplus money and that we're no longer hungry, I found a way out and nothing's stopping me, instantly I got addicted to fast currency. I'm dealing with nature's elements in housing developments trying to stack dead presidents.

There was no rehab, I had it bad, I'm breaking night after night, eyeballing my stashed zip lock bag. Life was a bitch for me and my homies, our situation was almost identical, I shared wealth with them all instead of going for self . . . a bunch of poverty-stricken kids created a full get-money circle. Wants became a thing of the past, we bought cars

Albert 'Infinite the Poet' Carrasco

when kids our age was pumping gas, we traveled to change bad weather forecast. We could possess anything we desired, that was a "pro" the "con" is . . . to maintain that lifestyle, most of my homies expired. I grew up drinkn ponche made with Malta, now as a game survivor, I pour out champagña for my dead pañas.

The Last Soldier of Poverty

I walked on half-good and half-broken tiles in my apartment's hall, had holes where knobs should be on doors, besides my cereal boxes and kitchen cabinets, there was spiders spinning webs and roaches parlaying on my wall. My neighbors had phones . . . not us, you had to call my fam out the window to see if we were home.

My living room furniture was a lumpy and saggy love-seat and crates with twelve-inch records on them as little tables, a ten-inch tube television with a hanger or foil for antennas, but there still was so much snow it looked like all shows were shot in the winter.

It was embarrassing in the beginning when I had to knock on doors with . . . can I borrow food notes, but I got used to it and started forging numbers, instead of asking for two eggs, I wrote four, instead of a cup of rice, I changed it to a few cups, instead of four slices of bread, it'll be eight . . . I got smart and guaranteed the next day's breakfast and dinner.

My kool aid was faucet water ice cubes and a pound of sugar, we put bread crumbs on free government cheese bricks, fried it and made cheddar stix in the brix, that was when we could get our hands on them because they went fast in the slums. That all changed when I grabbed my first pack. I felt money, so there was no coming back, for protection I copped my first gat, from the floor up I helped build a trap.

I'm eating, comfortably living and resting, rooftop bottle and can aim testing, I'm mobile now, got a few bills of sales for sales, stashed a few bills for bail, bought gold and diamonds to pawn and get back up when I fell and when all else failed. Wants became a thing of the past from hand to handing the contents of a Pyrex glass.

Albert 'Infinite the Poet' Carrasco

I made my own wishes come true, so did my crew, we went from poverty to wealthy, we're splurging hard body, from fighting evictions, we went to weed-spots to party and bars to look like stars spending rent money daily. Cash was more important than worrying about who's going to be the first to bid or die, after the first went to jail and the first one died, maintaining financial freedom was something we continued to try.

One two three four five kites, one two three four five faces taped on walls over crates and cardboard to prevent the wind from blowing out the fire on wicks and disturb the deceased makeshift mural candle lights. I had an army at the end, if I didn't have fiends all around me, I would've been a lonely soldier of poverty.

The Lyrical Dealer

Mom wasn't smoking but I'm a crack baby, dad died so the hood raised me, dealing with misdemeanors selling felonies brought out the felon in me, in da school of hard knocks my major was ghetto home economics . . . kitchen chemistry. Cause of the way I whipped contents of a Pyrex glass, I graduated head of my class. I was on the block advertising color tops trying to make ends meet since Ramo threw up hip hop don't stop in beat street, since bambaataa and the Zulu nation jams in bronx river, since the days of guardian angels used to go at it with black sheep. I know the streets well; bags are permanent under my eyes cause of all those broken nights making power moves to keep every pocket in my fatigues swell. I got caught up young, as soon as I got introduced to the white girl, I was sprung; at fifteen, was in Spofford for a gun; at sixteen, was a shooting victim; at forty-three, I mourn many sons. I saw the beginning and ending of many hustlers run, some by death or life in state and federal detention. When it comes to survivors, there's only a few, most of those young men walk round like they got Alzheimer's, they've been around for years but now they don't remember you. They're veterans of misfortune, soldiers of bad times, eighties' allies that lost their mind. A few can't come to the hood because the streets say they're no good, every set got green lights to terminate on sight, so they creep through sewers, avoiding the lime light, so the guns don't spark puncturing their body like paper and pegs from a litebrite. I roll thru the bx with deuces raised like . . . buenos Dias . . . was da borough prez before Ruben Diaz . . . wore my gold teeth and carried my snub trey eight just in case hell serenades like a young version of Ruben blades. My name holds weight like ballers connects, although I left the trade the respect is still there like if I'm infinitely made cause I never left the hood, it's just that in the winter I stay in the shadows and in the summer under shade keeping up with modern day Urbana.

Infinite Poetry

This young tigere grew into a titere, a weed-Tere, a hustler puttn oj's on hold to go to broadway to cop ye before it was okay for most to come out without a parent to play. I was a pusher's prey, poor, smart and brave, I fit the criteria to raise figures as a money slave.

Hey Al, you want to take off those beat-up karate slippers or those beat up chancletas, if you're tired of the rice and eggs or Mac and cheese alone for dinner, export soda galletas with butter for snacks and sugar water for a chaser, take this, advertise it, it'll make both our lives better, I said say no more, for decades after that first day hell serenaded, I was dirty when I walked out my project door.

I stood strapped with 'bout two or three gats walking the trap collecting profit from packs and to let the hood know to fall back, Tati quieto homies, got a tat that says touch me and die . . . respect the art work wo-dee or it'll be a big chance you'll have a mouthful of maggots in a casket eternally clocking z's and I don't even gotta bust mine's, you'll get done dirty by my man ICU and flatline, if them two get hit that's when I'll go to into the waistline to get mine, in the streets what separates life from death was a thin line.

I used to shave rock to fill vials, then chop rock to fill slabs, I had to use the sealer for stealers and constantly check to see if dudes opened, tapped it, then resealed it with a lighter. I was on my job cause that was exactly what it was to me, it was my nine to five but I did sixteen hours overtime daily, so twenty-four seven, I was on drug havens, around shooting galleries and crack houses, richness craving.

I was poor then rich, fell then blew, fell then blew, I was going up and down like a pogo stick in the bricks, every time

I got ahead of the game, the outcome would be the same, the saved gains went to funeral directors, lawyers, bails and bond after raids and sweeps for members of the crew. A lot of time went playing catch up because dudes kept getting murdered and caught up, I've seen blood on floors and walls looking like ketchup and constantly waited on lines outside criminal and supreme, when two twenty charges were brought up.

This went on so long dudes got sent up the river for ten, fifteen and twenty years, came home and got right back in the lineup of their old hustling peers, then shortly after . . . they got sent back up the river or looked down the barrel of their life-ender. I had to open my eye and think out the trap, hmmm . . . if this cycle keeps happening, I'll be left without nothing like when I first started minus a lot of good friends that sadly and untimely departed.

Reinventing myself was detrimental to my remaining homies and my health, I did what very few men got to do, I quit, I retired so I don't gotta hear, sorry INF, he expired. I had to build a platform so we all could eat off, my passion for writing came into use, while on hiatus I thought to myself . . . why not save those on the come up and the youth? I can destroy the facade and reveal truth because I am living proof that we were tightening our own noose.

Ten years later . . . Infinite the fiery Phoenix from the bricks, the ex-kitchen Pyrex chemist emerged. My urban wordplay quickly put me up with the rest of the street life protégé griots.

I go hard in the paint on the streets of New York like a rigor body outlined in chalk, I'm a pro-bono teacher in the school of hard knocks, hot blocks, ya know for those skiing on blow till they bump into their killer or the dees like Bono and trees.

Now I'm an author, I'm trying to make it to be a best-seller so I can help my family and the families of all my brothers. In time, I expect to be in documentaries shown on all channels on tv, maybe a broadway play called "the life of ye", then the big screen, no actors, all the remaining guys from team will play themselves, I'll get the sons from the ones that are no longer here to play their father. I emotionally spit, write emotional scripts, hopefully, I'll get that opportunity and live past sixty so I can break bread with those that got forty-five to click . . .

Albert 'Infinite the Poet' Carrasco

Time Flew

Time flew . . . I guess that's why they call it the fast life. We went from being poor, asking momma for a dollar to hear, from where? Do you want 100 pelos from my chocha? . . . I heard that same phrase when visiting my friends from their mother . . . That was a dramatic way of saying . . . no, stop asking and to go away. We were poor and young, where there was a will there was a way . . . we had that will, we walked from the sound view then back to castle hill with a bag full of empty aluminum cans for 5 cents refunds. At that time, there was no pride involved, it was fun. That would be our curriculum, we didn't care, we knew when we were halfway through the month there was absolutely no chance of getting money, ask your mother . . . na, ask yours . . . no one would dare . . . that's life growing up on welfare.

Summer youth came along, that would be the only job many of my friends would ever have, I remember every two weeks we cashed them checks, you couldn't tell us nothing, we walked around as if we were rich in the projects because having more than twenty dollars in our pocket was just a wish, a hundred was a dream come true, I still remember the faces of excitement sported by my crew. Every pay day, we went to Jew man to cop a pair of airs and some gear, our last checks was spent on Delancy so we could buy chuckers and leathers for winter. We did that for a few summers . . . those were the good ole days.

The mid-eighties came, along with it came the recipe for cooked cain, because wealth died along with my father, it was a way to ease hunger and poverty pains, not yet knowing it would bring in others. The product was introduced to me, I introduced it to my brothers, we became a hustling posse eager to make money against the wishes of our usually single mothers and to replace the earnings of our deceased, deadbeat and divorced fathers. The local park was where we handled our business, we sat under signs that say "park closes at dusk", morning noon and night until packs were finished. Just like that we got sucked in, not too long before that, the park was actually used for recreation instead of a spot where us street dreaming apprentices thought we could make millions.

A few hundred dollars every two weeks could no longer cut it, after a while of learning the ropes if you gave us coke, we'll cook it or if you gave us dope, we'll cut it, we became project kids with no budget. We had drivers when we shopped, runners to cop, oversea connections that cropped ready to shipment drop, poverty was a thing of the past and it would continue to be like that as long as fiends needed main vein injections or a blast . . . so we thought. It did last, but through the years, many passed, some went to jail and will never again see the ave, some survivors are not in the same mind-state as me, I see symptoms of early Alzheimer's in some old timers and hurt and pain in the eyes of others.

Money-Hungry

I remember being in the kitchen chef'n bombs, trying to finish up before getting busted by moms. When I heard her key enter the tumbler, it was over, I would run down that project hall to my bedroom door like a runner back with a stiff arm making sure that glass didn't crack, then act like I'm gonna take a shower but I'm really in the bathroom to finish the process with two bic lighters. I couldn't let her catch me, but at the same time, I had to do what I had to do, I was money-hungry. Behind closed doors, I was living another life, literally. To ease hunger pains, I said yes to the offering of cocaine. Did the pain ease? Na, I would've rather died of starvation than to feel the hurt I feel because of the reaper and his army of soul thieves. I'm scarred to my core, sometimes when I write what I saw, my pen cries and my eyes get sore, I would tear but there's no more salt water in my ducts after weeping for my father. Verbal and written expression releases decades of built-up tension, my inner self burns in super nova, if I didn't spit Amoebas, paramecium and Protozoa, I'll probably go through spontaneous combustion. While trying to save lives, I'm preserving my own, all the time I spend delivering mathematics, I'm preventing knives, revolvers, semis and fully automatics destroying my home.

Realness

I've always been considered a misfit, my style is unorthodox, peeps ain't used to hearing an ex-hustler turned poet spit out the box. Females aren't bitches, my dudes aren't my niggers, my pants don't sag for swag. my third eye has bionics, I'm hooked on phonics but I choose to mix laymen with Ebonics so I can reach them dough boys on the corner and give 'em a higher learning as they blaze piff kush and chronic somewhere low key as they push contents of a Pyrex or that medicine for the monkey in the projects. I'm hardcore . . . one of the best in a game of pawns like if this is Detroit and my name is les, I son dudes like Seth, these Ralph tresvie mr. sensitivity homies are Ashley to me. Inf is bona fide nonfiction writer, dude's comical, funny brothers like the chocolate droppa, the lemniscate is urbanas betta cappa, like a choppa on full auto I pop bar after bar like two-taped bananas. If you're an artist from or coming to the rotten manzana, come see me, I'll put the word out and get ya a pass to tour NYC safely, I'm positive, the name is heavy, and in these NY streets if u don't know nobody, you'll get dirty . . . quickly.

I spit reckless at will, I'm burning pages, melting keys and bodying mics for landfill. Imma ghost, some dudes you hear ain't real, they're Casper, fakers, thug life impersonators, they're only as hard as my passed-off scriptures. I'm not arrogant, I just spit facts, fill-ins and fiction is irrelevant when I write about gats packs, traps and dead presidents. The lemniscate is OG in the boogie down like the clown, the hood knows me, been in the streets since malacos was the breakfast spot for my comrades from the Watson family, since the days of the pizza shop in the blvd to break bread with the g's from the bully, since I was buzzn horse shoe to horse shoe from CHP to cozy on my eighty, banshee, or something shinny driving through or around sound view

Albert 'Infinite the Poet' Carrasco

park to politic with born, q and petey. Since the days of me, scoobie, manny and baby B was short shifting g60's on 95 to Harlem or the major Deegan for a pit stop at beef and broc or triangles from Branson.

Street Wars

I went to war with sets and crews in the streets that showed me love because of them violating one of my peeps . . . it's the rules of engagement, once slugs fly trust goes bye bye, I'll never sleep as I walk in the jungle made by concrete. Inf is a Leo, king of beast, if you were placed on the menu, I'll feast . . . it's called loyalty, when my mans and them have a problem it's my problem . . . it becomes hereditary.

The hood respects my g, respects my family's metal tai chi mortal combat fatalities. We chaffed that fish scale and reina like farina and avena . . . inedible crema, ice water worked as a hardener, then we used gem stars to chop that ready rock like table top john Henry's. We filled tupperware after tupperware, CHP raised some urban coke heirs. My team was lethal rip to Ralphy Eddie Edgar bunca blue Kringle and my partna orlandito, they died young reppn bellaco . . . bendito.

There's many more that met their demise and fell so the team could rise. Hungry minorities lost lives trying to form a monopoly, we were apprentices, so some made moves that was sloppy, others learned from those mistakes that led to crimes scenes surrounded with yellow tape courtesy of homi, after that nobody made moves if an og didn't say copy. Attacking, overtaking, not even partying was right unless you were given a green light.

See, I chose to stay out of sight, made a few appearances in the day but roamed the bricks at night, I survived the time but I still send kites, visit prisons, send commissary and constantly visit cemeteries, I promised to ride or die so, I'm riddn with the incarcerated and praying to my homies that didn't make it. When I'm writing, it's murder ink; when I speak in spoken tongue, its redrum, nonfiction diction from

Albert 'Infinite the Poet' Carrasco

the life of the slums, drugs guns death murder and open cases from going on the run. I bring the ghetto to a stage near you, explain the life of knockn down rectangles like dominoes then walk off yelln capi cu.

The Power to Speak

I got the power to speak to the streets and have it listened because it understands me, my lingo, my dialect, plus the knowledge I bring from living life cooking that thing over the stove or scooping then scotch taping the glassine on the table. I was a wild individual living in the wilderness of evil, trying to make a reality of an old hereditary fable. I got bullet holes and stitches, arthritis and calluses from years of gripping the handle of Pyrex dishes and blue steel with infrared and tracers so there's no missing while I'm trying to achieve triple beam wishes.

I laid my head to rest with jeans, vest and my weapon on, they say when you get to the point of no return that your lost forever, well I was gone, dealing with aluminum foil dubs nicks of hard and bundles of her-on. I was like a doctor on twenty-four-hour standby, I took calls for work at all hours, I just didn't have the knowledge to perform a tracheostomy on my homies so they could breathe after choking on blood from a drive-by.

The hood is not good with sideline advice, I don't care if you graduated suma cum laude, magnum cum laude, got your bachelors or masters, you're still blind death and dumb to the life I lived and the way of life at this very moment of many others if you never mixed powders in boiling water, if you never saw the addiction of a mother or father copping in plain view of sons and daughters, then years later those same children that copped with mom and dad got it bad, sucking the glass dick, constant pricks for a main vein hit, if you never faced the trial and tribulations, afflictions and oppression we've faced for years, you can't give lessons to me or my peers, what you say will go through one ear and out the other, what I recite marinates in the minds of my brothers.

Albert 'Infinite the Poet' Carrasco

I scribe the steps of fate of the now late, so personas and consciousness can have a life and death debate on situations that lead to wakes, funerals, burials and the loss of the yearly tradition of cutting a birthday cake. I am a ray of hope to the young Rey's and reina's caught up in the life of guns, coke, pills, and dope.

Lyrical Deterrent

I talk about my hard knock life with hopes of deterring kids from accepting pusher offerings as an escape from poverty option. When I was in the street looking for individuals to move material and they took it, it was up to them to understand the consequences of living dirty, you might go to prison or return to the essence for pitching what was given by kitchen chemist, we wouldn't warn ya, that's not the duty of a hustler, our job was to get rich, new jacks got thrown in the fire while big dogs sat home waiting for the day they could retire . . . ain't that a bitch? It's facts. These youngens think connections love them until all hell breaks loose like losing all the re-up money in a raid, connects don't care they'll put your head in a noose if they're not paid . . . no matter what you think that's the truth, I'm trying to educate the youth, I'm here to explain that the game isn't friendly, it's deadly and I hear dudes always talk 'bout how they'll ride and die but I see through them, I know those who aren't ready, somebody just put a battery in them, I call 'em ever-ready's, the ones that get put in the "why me" for crying cause they facing a felony, forget if they hear they're going to supreme for trial, they'll become suicidal. I've seen dudes drop weapons and roll when their teammates are taking fire, there's many that act gangsta only cause they've never had real drama, they drop the Ebonics, the blunt mixed with loud and chronic, straighten up their bop, forget 'bout fast life gwop and move out of New York after seeing a friend or foe with gunshot head trauma. Just because you're broke, dirty and hungry, don't think the game is good money . . .

Albert 'Infinite the Poet' Carrasco

Scars

I stare at my bullet holes and think how lucky I was, I open my draw and see so many funeral cards that I can play "I declare war". It's sad to say that, with a few more, I'll be able to throw them in the air and pick up fifty-two dead men off the floor. That'll be disrespectful, so of course, I really won't do that, I'm just trying to get my point across by showing how death came back-to-back in the trap. I got cards of young kids, teenagers and older men, they all died by the knife or gun for dealing with a traditional curriculum in the slums. That's hand to handing cooked white lines like minority-colored mimes, the difference is we weren't silent we shouted color advertisements around housing developments to collect dead presidents, a few survived the storm, a lot are resting underground to never again deal with the season's elements. At times, I feel as if I was chosen to teach through urban spoken, I guess while really living the life of a hustler, I was actually being educated to give a higher learning on the life of boy mixers and girl boilers to misdemeanors that'll turn into felon repeaters, lifers or friend mourners if they follow the path of our forefathers like I did following my father. I got a chance to escape that atmosphere like a molecule of gas exiting the exosphere, so I write daily like it's poetry month 12 times a year as an urban savior. See, I'm not with fiction diction, this dictation comes from a nonfiction fact spitter, like when I say five out of ten hustling men will die, it's not an assumption it's prediction, pay attention to my street life lyrical simulation, over and over it has been written and I will continue writing as long as there is a drug market to cause gun clapping. My words won't stop shipments crossing borders but I could drop the sales on import by stopping my kin from becoming traffickers.

Urban Poetry Is My Life

Urbana is my life not a genre. I grew up poor, sold drugs, carried guns and witnessed the effects of murder in the slums, I was chosen to pull the plug on one of street life brothers because his mother and father didn't have the strength to do that to their son. I broke many nights in lobby's parks or corners with caps or slabs of all colors trying to fight poverty. Everywhere I went I carried a gun, now everywhere I go, I got a slug in me from another young felon that carried one.

I paint it so vivid cause I actually lived it, believe me when I write these bars, I reminisce and get livid, I mourn alone when I spit it, inf is the anti-reaper . . . he swings his scythe, I swing my pen and split it. I slam every day . . . my wisdom versus the devil's temptation, he used to beat me because I didn't understand, now that I over-stand I got the upper hand, our last run in, I extinguished his flame, our future battle's outcome will be the same, he knows that, so as much time I use in a day to right truth, he's trying just as hard to lie to our youth and to keep a hold on blind deaf and dumb grown men. Our battle has been televised . . . mine's on stage, the streets and social media, his is on the news, depression, murderers and kidnappers setting off alerts named after Amber . . . he gets a few hours a day in the lime light, I get twenty-four to shine bright and expose his dangers.

A Hit-Man

I hold my gats tight and wish for the opposite of gesundheit when I sneeze, ya know when I get atchooo.

When you're in my crosshairs,
it's man slaughter or murder . . .
Rigor mortis in blank stares.

Death is my livelihood.

I'll use a sweeper and put a hole in your stomach, reach my hand in and pull out your small intestines, stretching it twenty-three feet like I'm science testing . . . that's how I eat.

Everybody has a price for their head, if you pay it . . . there's no ifs ands or buts . . . they're dead.

The first time, I was scared, but it got easier and easier, I'm like a natural-born killer.

When I'm begged . . . no, don't do it, please . . . I take it like they don't want God and send them to hell, silence comes quick because I get peeved with yells.

Ordinary people will never see my face, to them I'm just a tale. I'm a hit man, hit man/ killer, killer.

If you committed a homicide . . . when we meet,
it's a hearse ride.

Eye for eye, cheek for cheek, they call me revenge, they call me payback, they call me to havoc wreak.

Killers murdered so many friends of mine . . . that made me a soulless freak.

I went insane, laughter became the emotion of hurt and pain. I go to sleep in agony and wake up waiting to create tragedy.

Twenty-four hours a day, I'm in hysterics, remembering the faces of mourning families.

Today it's a drug dealer, tomorrow it's a rapist, the day after it's a robber, then a kidnapper, then a drunk driver . . .

I have two days of the week empty, I'm available for offers.

There're others like me, but we don't step on each other's toes because the world is a huge market to profit off woes.

We'll retire when there's no one else to expire, so I guess we'll have lucrative jobs forever.

Remember . . . after you commit the ultimate felony, you're prey as soon as the hardest mourner pays. Signed the hit man, hit man/ killer, killer . . .

Shootout

Please baby, I need you here with me, if you love me, you won't leave. (The door opens and slams shut). She stands there, bawl'n until she collapsed into a heap of woes as if someone removed her skeleton.

We out! (The car waiting outside speeds off.)

You sure you saw him, right? Yeah, he walked past me, aaight lets go huntn. (They're driving block to block slowly, respecting all traffic rules cause they're dirty.)

There he goes! Drive to the corner and let me out. I'm coming with you! Na, keep the car idling, there's no need for two of us to get caught, besides we only need one of us to do what I'm going to do. (He gets out, gun in hand and uses parked cars as stealth.)

(The driver) Ohhh shit, beat walkers! A yo c-ciphers! (It's too late.)

(Gunshots ring out in broad day.) Got you, motherfucker, that's pay backs for my brother! (He turns, runs making his way back to the whip.)

(Beat walkers' radio in for back up as they run towards the gunfire.) Freeze! (He runs the opposite way with gun still in his hand. He quickly thinks) . . . I shoot for freedom, get life or they're going to take my life . . . Blam blam blam (he bangs at the cops . . . the cops bang back.)

(The driver sees they got his man pinned, so he opens fire.) Blammmmmmmm, (fully auto fire backs them down). Mo, let's go! Blammmmmmmm (he makes it to the car.)

Mo, we're fucked, hear all the sirens and the gun shots! (Nonstop shots are ringing off from all directions.) Peel! (They drive off cops in pursuit.) They setup road blocks, we gotta get out and make into one of the buildings.

(They stop and jump out.) Blammmmmmmmm blam blam blam blammmmmm (it's a war zone.) Hurry up son, get in the building. What the fuck are you doing! I'm calling my man . . . Ayo shit, got real, my man is coming open up for him sun, fuck outta here, I ain't leavn. I told you, there's no need for both of us to go down, besides you're my right-hand man, I need you to take care of my son, give me the choppa, run through the back of this building into the other, go to the roof and cross over, my homie is waitn for you on five. Nooo, please man please . . . (The driver leaves.)

Blammmmmmm blammmmmmm blammmmmmm (the entire precinct is firing back including swat.) Come out with your . . . blammmmmm (he goes out to his death).

(She's watching TV) Lord, please make sure my baby is safe, he's angry because his brother was murdered last week, now he's the only child I have left, losing him would make me absolutely weak . . . (breaking news) Beat walkers patrolling their area hear gun shot and run to investigate. Upon arrival, they see a man on the floor, appeared to be dead, and a man running from the scene with a gun in his hand. A shootout ensued, no cops were hurt, one suspect is dead and the driver of the getaway car escapes . . .) Wow, that's so crazy, when will these kids learn?

(The phone rings . . . it's the driver) I am watching the news, what are you telling me? (The phone drops.) Noooooo! Not my other baby!

The Hustler's Sons

My mom and pops mixed me with Puerto Rican rum and whiskey . . . uh . . . what a set off R.I.P. to biggie, it was euphoria when dad entered my mother, he came, she skeeted, seven months later premature infinite was being watched in an incubator. Dad knew he made a gangster from birth because I was a c section baby, he said that's a sign that his son is going to be far from punani.

He bred me to be a soldier, as I got older, if I ignored instruction or orders, I would have to kneel on rice in corners, when I cried and complained, he would just say . . . boy, be quiet and wipe that water, after a few punishments, I learnt how to deal with the pain till punish time was over. He had zero tolerance for disrespect. Where he went, I went. What he did, I saw, I listened to every conversation, a bloody lip would be the result of repeating or volunteering information, so I just sucked in words and visions as I stood at attention right next to him.

I explained to y'all in "military" how I wanted to go military school but when my father died that dream died. All the convos he had and all the things I saw him do became hereditary. My older brother already started hustln, now I'm that youngen roaming drug havens looking for a spot to pitch in cause now we don't have a pot to piss in. My mom . . . she didn't want any part of it, my brother would be going in and out she'll be catching fits, I kept my movements a little more discrete as I roamed the streets with treys and nicks.

Big bro relocated to Audubon, I stood in the hood packing bombs, where the older cats left off us young aristocrats carried on. Mom lost her husband and her two older sons, her husband to cancer, her sons to drugs, guns, buildings, lobbies and lucrative corners for that almighty dollar. Momma knew she couldn't do nada cause her offspring was raised by a spanish sergeant slaughter, the eina was our arena, every day scrambling was like a royal rumble, no clothes lines, pile drivers and buckles, it was every clique for themselves as we tried to evade projectiles disbursed from handguns or sub machine guns with suppressed or silent muzzles.

I let my mother down . . . when I got caught with the burner, she came to court pleading, "he's a good boy, your honor", since I was only fifteen, he granted me leniency, two weeks after the arrest I was released with an A.C.D. I could no longer lie to my mother, besides there was no way to hide that fast cheddar from her, I'm coming in with new kicks, fancy gear, gold on my neck and diamonds in my ears, I said, sorry mom but we live in poverty and I'm going to get us out of here.

Time passed . . . tic tock, like my running mates in the trap that stashed cooked rock in tube socks or zip locks with rice for that d-block. We all passed the point of no-return, addicted to mask and grinders or watching powder boil in water to an oil then to a solid that slowed down the process of blinking eyelids, we were doing what was taught or shown to us as kids growing up in the slums from New York. We were all hustlers' sons . . . now I hustle murder, jail, drugs and guns with my urban spoken tongue.

Albert 'Infinite the Poet' Carrasco

Concrete Imagery

My words hit hard, I'm the poster poet, a walking spoken billboard for drugs, guns and the lives of bidders in jail yards. I don't cuss, no need. I do make references from past experiences that are cursed indeed. I do say cocaine and dope that's the powders for main veiners and sniffers with numb noses and frozen throats. I do speak suicide, homicide and genocide fluently, I speak of roaches in a cereal box, mice droppings on countertops, two adults sharing a twin-size cot. rust marks on stainless steel pots, I'm a pro with the welfare system, court system, correction system, the rushing into emergency then to ICU curriculum, the morgue, the autopsy, the three days of viewing, then the burial of many men. I saw brains out of heads, intestines out stomachs, belts on pulleys lowering bodies s l o w l y. I know czars dying slowly being bars accumulating.

Swollen keloid scars . . . I got so many incarcerated, I go with a posse, so we can pull three men in the same jail for a visit. I can tell you how bastard kids feel, I can tell you how widows and widowers feel. I had a chance of being a valedictorian, now I'm a street life veteran, a hood life spoken mystorian, I say mystorian because his-story doesn't really teach about anything pertaining to the slums.

The Devil Had Me

The devil had me, I was a dumb deaf and blind fool, now I'm god's tool, blessing the world with jewels, every action has an equal and opposite reaction, I know the rules, so I teach them through wisdom, verbal manifestation of thoughts into sound, I wear my five-point crown, my linguistics are profound, I drop bombs like cyrax with every syntax,

On the life of passing road side bombs like in Iraq, had the sick open or itching like they had anthrax, dope or cracks I was trapped like rocks under a color cap, once you see that money there's no looking back, you'll get addicted to bagging on the table or to the system of shaving/chopping vial packing then Tupperware tossing them jacks, I lived in the ghetto but shopped at sax fifth avenue after I pc'd off hell's brew and whatever was left from paying for funerals, flowers, and spray-painted urban murals. Hey, young poor world, I know our struggles, I know how life feels so troubled, I know how it feels to burry somebody by hand, why do the young die young? I understand. I almost died early but it just wasn't my time, all my friends died during that time of crime, the path we were on was filled with land mines. We tried to walk stealthy to earn the title of wealthy now most are fossils for future archeology, or anchored in ameba and protozoa covered with algae. The game will seduce ya, you'll turn into a stationary cement object in the projects as if medusa stared at you. The world revolves, people evolve, we ran quickly to get out of poverty to no resolve, almost all involved returned to the essence, ashes to ashes, they redissolved, a harsh learnt lesson to those tired of having less than when bills were greater than what was offered by the government. Drugs become monetary supplements to have average or surplus while living in housing tenements. The hustlers and pushers will find you before you find a job, I know to some that sounds odd, but in the 80s, minimum wage was 3.35, in a drug shift you could make a thousand dollars, the weighing of the options wasn't hard when living in squalor as legal squatters. Us young guys with fire and desires in our eyes didn't realize that it's better to be poor outside than inside jail. we had to go to jail to realize how we failed, even then instead of going to the law library, they study their mistakes and the mistakes of other incarcerated individuals, max out, come home, repeat the same scenario hoping to be educated enough to prevail. After a few sales, they're right back in a cell as a repeat offender, one more strike makes them a three-time looser, now minor offenses come along with time in sentence.

Russian Roulette

Every day, I played Russian roulette minus the gun to my head, with all the risk and gambles I faced and took it was a high probability that I could've wound up dead, regardless to the fact I continued because there were family members that needed shelter and to be fed. My ideas and plans were the six-shot revolver spinning with five slugs revolving, acting them out was me pulling the trigger. I lived like that for years, luck was on my side, unfortunately it wasn't the same for my peers, they died early, cause of death was homicide but we were doing it to ourselves, death certificates should say "poor condition, thought process suicide". I walk the streets of New York and see many men with the same look I had when I was holding that barrel to my temple, I see them in front of me, on both sides of me through my peripheral, it's the faces of . . . any day, I could die, people, you won't be able to relate unless you've played Russian roulette. I see murderers, hustlers, stick up kids, muggers and robbers while they plan or commence with evil walking amongst prey, AKA ordinary people. It's like a gained sense.

I see hurt and pain mixed with fuck it's whatever thoughts on rotation in brains . . . I see through them . . . it's X-ray ex-felon vision. I'm going to start tagging my lemniscate symbol on buildings and walls to be seen as the resistance, I'm going to start writing pieces and quotes and staple them to trees like Christians do, so when they see my symbol or when they read my writings, they'll know that infinite is here to save them from the pestilence with persistence.

Albert 'Infinite the Poet' Carrasco

Bipolar

I used to think I was bipolar, as I grew older inner voices got clearer and clearer, now I know it was guidance from the crossed over, at first it was just one, my father, then so many, it was hard to focus on one speaker, that's because all my friends would be talking over each other. It took some time but I learned how to hone in on dad's or any one of my kin's conversations, so I can give them my undivided attention. I'll rather have them here with me, although they're not physically, mentally, they never leave me lonely. They hear what I hear, they see what I see, sound and visions cast to the heavens automatically. When I don't know if I should go left or right, I close the two to see darkness, to see light. I become a vessel, I ride shotgun, while they control hell on earth navigation. I know they want me with them, but they know my purpose on the blue planet with a red surface. I'm a poetic archeologist here to unravel the past to spit the art-of-facts, my words can help prevent you from becoming skeletal remains mark by boulders with your name when I spit the game . . .

A Lost Boy

I planned for my future but never thought I would live to forty, the average life span of the hustling man was twenty, so I gave myself the benefit of the doubt and prepared to be around till I was thirty, that preparation stopped ten years too early, by this time I thought my mother and brothers would be mourning me, looking at old pictures with their hands clasped in prayer, tied together with rosary's, comforting each other by saying, "no worries family, he's with daddy".

It's amazing to me how I was ready to die, I thought of the view looking down as my soul was soaring to the sky, I already soaked in the looks of teary eyes, I already saw my plot reading "here lays A.C. He was gunned down in a blood bath", every day, I opened my eyes to the am sun, I lived like it was my last before succumbing to the gun in the slums while I chased e pluribus unum.

I did the evil that men do to earn blood residuals, kept the toast at my hip, back pockets, had extra extended clips as I claimed the strip pushing five-dollar hits, I was trying to make a killing cause there was a big probability that the next day I would no longer be living. So, I was sacrificing myself, giving myself up like lent so after my death momma can still pay her rent.

Thirty came and I'm still alive, I'm lost, the game is over, my saved money is depleting what skills do I have other than being a crime boss? I was confused . . . did the devil like the work I did on hell's surface or was I being saved for a higher purpose? Reality was scary, I didn't plan for this, the coward way out would've been puttn one in my head or slittn my wrist but no cowardly blood runs through me, so I wasn't going to blast or cut myself, I had to create a plan b, that was the reinvention of A.C.

Albert 'Infinite the Poet' Carrasco

Digging in thought, I honed in on a talent that went hidden due to the life I was living . . . that was drawing and writing. Now, I paint pictures with literature, when it comes to the white girl, I write portraits like the painter of the Mona Lisa, when it comes to murder, I ink redrum all over because I felt the pain of losing my brothers when I was supposed to be their keeper, now I'm the alchemist spitting golden bars on the life of kitchen chemist and those that returned to the essence.

When and How?

I remember wondering how and when would I die in the drug game, would it be a set up? A stick up? A home invasion, kidnapped, tied up then taken to another location, so the kidnappers can hold me for ransom? If that was the case, I know they still would've murdered me after getting the currency, because if they would've set me free, they knew their only chances of survival would've been to leave the country and hope not to be spotted by allies of the family. My homies and people I knew was dying left and right, so I wore Kevlar and carried guns day and night, prepared for a gunfight and to evade a murderous plight. I lived every day like it was my last, smoked massive grass, constantly went to strip clubs to look at tits and ass, went to bars and made sure I never had an empty glass, I had to party hard before I passed, that was my mentality daily chasing dirty money on the ave. I used to constantly visit and keep myself around the ones I loved because at any given time I know I could've been symbolized by a dove. They knew that too. They knew my life was expendable in the pursuit of residuals. I knew they loved me cause they used to cry while telling me that they rather have me poor and alive than trying to get rich by making cocaine rise and die. I would tell them, don't worry about me, then wipe their eyes before saying bye, it would hurt them because they didn't know if that bye was till later, tomorrow or forever . . . What was crazy is that I didn't know which of the three it would be either. I no longer wonder and my love ones no longer tear on departure cause that life is over.

Albert 'Infinite the Poet' Carrasco

Fossil-Fueled

I'm fueled by the loss of my friends . . . that's kids and young men, the first to die was 16 in the 80s, the last passed in 2013 three years short of being 50, in-between the tally is close to 2 dozen, that's a lot of motivation. Just call me the male whoopi of poetry . . . what you read and hear are visions and sounds of too many swayzies. I narrate the life of the crossed over to the future, infinite is a ghost writer for ghost riders. I see gore in my mind like survivors from the invasion Normandy, when it comes to deadly bars, I am an anomaly because there's no way to erase bloody memories . . . they haunt me. My mind is scarred like the outer body of Jim Carey in twenty-three. I'm focused on spreading wisdom on hell's surface, so I dig deep then spit with purpose for those in the trap, painting the town red like cool g rap, beating state charges like nothing, feeling they're untouchable until they get investigated by the Feds and face numbers that are double or triple digits, or until they meet the reaper and get fitted for inexpensive caskets. When I spit it, I'm prolife like the protesters with pictures in front of abortion clinics with the mind state of mourning mothers or weeping widows, rusting windowpanes with tears of pain, thinking about the first time they held their children and the first day they met their husbands. I'm one of the realest, not a theorist, I was born in the game. Dudes came, saw and was forced to leave like scared tourists or like chefs from Hell's Kitchen that couldn't stand the heat in these New York streets, so they really can't bring raw reality, they just recite what they discovered as being temps in the coke, dope, gun murder industry. I saw many men rise and fall, those men that lived blinded but brave hearted . . . I don't see them no more, they're dead or locked up forever after your honor banged his gavel on the table like the mighty Thor does to floors.

A Diamond in the Ruff

Don't mean mug me, I've been shot, so I walk around paranoid, we ain't gonna face fight but I will deliver a buck fifty nike keloid scar, I get along with everybody but plz don't cross me, cause I'll place you as the target in my crosshairs' homie, the only cross ya wanna see from me is with my arms letting ya know where home-town be, inf be the poetic Curtis Jackson, I'll grab the mic and declare war with anybody, in this sport there's no rules, I got that murder ink that'll end careers like ja rule. Dudes are jokers, I'll rip 'em from ear to ear so they could look happy as I instill fear.

I'm 'bout that life and I fit the stereotype . . . I'm Puerto Rican and I'm good with a knife, better hope that donors went to blood banks and donated your blood type. I walked around with a gem by my cheek, a gat by my hip, and a two-shot derringer in my high-top sneaks. Where I'm from, the streets are dangerous, I watch everything in slow mo like I puffed angel dust, being cautious from brothers trying to make me famous instead of maintaining my infamous stature. To me, everybody walking pass me is a murderer, before they take me from my mother that killer is gonna need a coroner, then just for rec I'll go to their wake, let off a clip in the corpse to make it do the uptown shake, so please, when you see me, don't make movements suddenly cause that'll be something you'll dread, one false move . . . boom, bye bye, that baddy boy dead.

Think ya the one neo? Tira la Pecho, ay bendito lo siento mucho, you're food for my dogs bien probecho. Yolo . . . you only live once, so if it ain't natural, I'm not givn lames a chance. I'd rather be bunkies with my brother Peter rollack than to get caught slipping due to my past of selling rock. All I do is step on stage and set the shit ablaze, I'm t h c for the stoners, soft and hard cocaine for the sniffers/bassers and heron for the main vein works penetrators, I got that 187-duct tape flow for murderers and home invaders, I can drop the Ebonics and rhyme proper in laymen's for the intellectuals, hieroglyphics for Egyptians and some out of this world material for extraterrestrials . . . I got something for every individual.

Yup, it's the eighth wonder, the lemniscate is on fire, I'm a diamond in the rough, dug up by miners in the Sierra Leone, wiped of the plasma to make my shine clearer, now I teach a die-alect like Rosetta, it's called stone. See, I'm a survivor from a hustling regime where wealth was weighed on triple beams while perusing the American dream. Whether it was girl or boy, the team was on the block with that gangster lean, cash ruled everything around us, then one by one we were marked in chalk in an area while friends and family had to stay on the perimeter of homicide crimes' scenes.

Inf was a hard knock scholar, graduated magnum bang loudly; that's the slums equivalent to magnum cum laude, now I'm a professor of Urbana in the rotten manzana. When I scribe on white lines, it's pure genius like my government followed by Einstein, some go hard in the paint . . . I'm turpentine, I bleed my heart out daily as if every day is valentine, I spread love on the life where youngens are symbolized as flying doves, I've lost so many its fucked up to say that at times it's hard to count all I know is through the years I earned a pet shop discount, I bought birds from fathers, they retired, so I built a relationship with his son, that's how many succumbed to the knife or gun on our get rich run in the slums. Everything I've witnessed from the two g's back to eighty-four is the reason why this Leo's roar is raw, puree, nonfiction word play on the life of ye.

I Am Living Proof of Change

I was a happy kid . . . life hadn't fucked me up yet. My only problems were smelling my big bro's feet when was asleep, having to blow game cartridges if I wanted to play Nintendo with my peeps and thinking I was too old at ten to hold mom's hand while crossing streets. That's about it. If I wasn't in gumball alley bmx'n, I was in the project's apartment hopp'n, ralphys, the comachos, orlandos, chachos, po's hector lebrons, max, cheese and sandro's . . . those were the usuals. My only need for money was when I heard mr. softy's jingle, when I wanted chino's, pizza and soda or lucky five roast beef and cheese hero's . . . life was sweet.

Fast forward two years . . .

What do you mean, he's dead? Na, my father's death-proof, I was so naive at twelve but being one of his pallbearers, I unwillingly dealt with the truth. Mom stretched dad's money the best she could . . . VA checks stopped, SSI stopped, we weren't doing too good. See, mom is my heartbeat.

Wasn't gonna let her go solo on food clothing and shelter, so I roamed the street. Dad passed in the year of the introduction of cooked Coke, I was trying to meet it, ayo I need blow! Their response would be "get the fuck outta here" as if I was a joke, I searched for that one chance, it was offered, I never looked back, not a glance. The "block" build-up started. One fiend two fiends, pack PC changed to grams on triple beams, my sandbox friends became a hustln team, just like that I'm in deep and nothing's going to take me out the streets, it's too late, now I know how to make cream. Dudes I asked for a come-up throw numbers around, I act interested then turn them down, fall back and watch me get rich, clowns. Death after death, bid after bid, I've gotten much older but I was still doing what I started as a kid.

Albert 'Infinite the Poet' Carrasco

Three decades later . . .

I walked away from it all . . . but . . . if I want to visit my friends, it's a trip to a correctional facility or to a cemetery, my sandbox homies are no longer around, so much went down. My mom went to jail because of me, her man tone went to jail for me, my big bro Sid . . . altogether, he lost twelve years for me, I have bullet holes and a slug in me, I'm filled with anger because of vivid memories, I pick up a pen and write blood to prevent other mes, it won't be easy because other "infinites" warned infinite and infinite ignored them, they were twenty, thirty years my senior, now that I'm forty four, the only way to let them know that they were right is through prayer, since I'm still here, I'll keep dropping bombs religiously, writing and reciting ghetto psalms as lessons to the new era. Life was good, then it became a bitch, it would've stood that way if I didn't find my niche.

His-story Repeats

When I opened up, it wasn't to blow up, it was to stop my stomach from aching so bad that I would liquid throw up. I wanted to fill the cabinets in momma's kitchen, so I did compra with my profit from nickel and dime pitchn. When cabinets were filled and I didn't have to worry 'bout nourishment, I got sucked into materialistic items like clothes and jewelry, bikes fitted with Vance and Hines, cars outed, tuned with chips and cams, turbo and g charged engines with small pulleys for faster revolution, you'll find me on 87 or 95 switchn the short shifter merkn, in-between gears you hear suction like my wip was sponsored by dyson.

Then I got caught up deeper, I can eat whenever! I had to stay dip-laced in something original, preferably leather, had keys to hydroplane in speed lanes from horsepower and melted Z rated pirellis. I got addicted to that fast life currency, I advertised my product on the surface of hell to gain clientele, I wanted to monopolize with my brothers, my ghetto soldiers, blocks were hot but we still walked through the fire trying to form an empire . . . greed took over.

Needs turned to wants, wants turned to cases and caskets for drug traffic. Death was a deterrent to some, it just made me go harder in the slums . . . I would say to myself, "Inf, don't stop now, rep the way you know how since you were a child, you can't turn away, they didn't turn back" . . . I married the game, my alter was a lobby courtesy of nycha. I held on to the trap, recruiting new hustlers and those known to bust their gats, them new dudes started to bid and get wigged, history was repeating, same scenes just another mother looking at her seed laying lifeless as he bleeds.

I went on visitations to the same jails with different wives holding crying toddlers cause they didn't want to leave their father, the days of yesterday were being replayed over and over, incarceration, burials and cremation became a part of the hustling culture. I found a different way to rep my brothers and teach others, I got friends and fans from New York, Asia to Africa recognizing our hard knock life, how we went from poverty to Attica, how very little are still alive struggling to survive and how the rest went to the father. I retired cause so many expired. I'm hoping these youngens read or hear me and understand what transpired and get inspired from the wisdom I've acquired to open third-eye lids.

Shattered Dreams

I came into the spoken word game to share knowledge on the life of murder and cain, I go hard not to claim fame but to represent the heaven sent that perished from hell on earth's fame. Infinite is a mourning griot. I miss my kin that was taken away, that's why when it comes to ye word play, I carpe diem . . . seize the day. I call this pain purple rain, cause this is what it sounds like when thugs cry, when thugs die, I spit wisdom, and go through perspiration but water never falls from my eye.

It's nothing about ego or testosterone, it's just after my father died, my ducts went dry to bone. Without tearing, the hood knew I was crying cause slugs would be flying. I got tired of seeing my men being lowered in the dirt but they kept on dying. Getting used to death isn't a good thing . . . I'm used to it, so I now cherish every moment with my friends like it's my last because there were times, I was with my men one minute, then a few minutes later I'm getting calls saying they've passed.

Most of my days I deal with the pain, then there's other days when I can't compress it in, so I visit the graves of my kin and talk to 'em . . . guys, please guide me, show me the right direction, help me with decisions, send me a sign that you're here with me listening! We grew up poor in a bad time. The Reagan era, bricks upon bricks were shipped across water with a deadly recipe that shocked and awed urban communities in many cities.

Crack . . . the party drug of 83 and 84 turned into the most addictive drug I ever saw before. These partiers were no longer partying they started selling their body or robbing to bass or make coolies and woolies from rock and shake from baking soda-risen cookies. They got caught up in a condition called addiction, they're stealing from parents, begging for money from friends and family, they multitasked . . . cause at the same time, they neglected their husbands or wives and children.

All hustlers were hustling for supremacy and ownership of corners, bodegas and lobbies to control the flow of phlebotomy currency. Users and pushers were constantly returning to the essence, new fiends and new hustlers' faces were now present. See, I left the game and haven't looked back since . . . not even a glance, but still till this day, if you offer a poor brother a million dollars for their soul after two three or years, two or three years later they'll be some weeping mothers. The thought of being rich overshadows the reality of death. It's 2014 and it's still the same way. Although the game is tabu. every day I walk the streets I see déjà vu, the same game, just different crews. History is repeating over and over, I guess infinite will be writing forever as the bearer of I'll street blues . . .

Self-destructive Adolescence

Youngens are still popping, youngens are still dropping, they're not even busting for funds, they're busting for fun, that's only until their own red runs from redrum by one of man's number one genocidal weapons. There're cameras all over watching these blind young brothers blaze at each other. They see where they came from, where they ran, or they can zoom in on the plates of the car that was driven. You're not low . . . it's a new era, dudes ain't just got a relationship they're on popo's payroll, homicide is getting notified by the local c.i's as soon as a dude dies.

Kids are becoming killers . . . in jail, they're scratching their head confused with what the judge said, "life", a sentence handed to them that's equivalent to being dead or healthy on a death bed. They don't realize this when the guns are being sparked for fame, ya know, an under-eye tear drop for everybody they claim. They're either laying in a casket with hands crossed holding crucifix's like tradition . . . or in a cell or yards reminiscing on what they're missing, wishing they could've been sentenced to electrocution instead of a lifetime dealing with correction institution repetition.

Yo yo, little brothers, watcha out here tryn to discover? Don't you read and hear my ether? My trap crack? My lyrical THC that'll get ya high like stoners rolling in wraps, games, dutchies, bambu or rizla paper? I'm trying to save y'all, pay attention to my nonfiction instead of those street-life Nostradamus predictions. It saddens me that these kids have no ambition, no drive, no desire to extinguish hell's fire, they rather cosign the liar, sell their soul just to get a rep and to get higher. There're many minds of Manson, evil-filled craniums ready to lift a brotha up like helium just because he ain't feeling him, they don't like his swag nor the block he's from, it's a curriculum of hate, embedded in neglected non-directed sons.

Some guys get a hard on seeing lights flashing, sirens blaring, bodies lying under a mother that's yelling while they're looking out the window with the lights turned off in the slums admiring their destruction. To put fear in the heart of their shorty they call them to turn on the tv, and brag . . . that body was me. For a reputation, they tell friends . . . that body was me. For respect, they let the streets know . . . that body was me. Then they cry out "woe is me, woe is me" to their family, so they can get them a private attorney, so they don't blow trial with a legal aid or eighteen b. Dudes want to bang, then rip sheets in cells and hang.

Mother and Son

Mother. I would rather be poor and have you with me forever rather than living temporarily rich till you go to prison or till you're laid in a ditch. Not being able to hold you, touch and kiss you would kill me inside, I think I'll die, if I ever get a knock on the door by homicide.

Son. Forgive me mother, but I need to make change, not e pluribus but surplus presidential paper. I need to change our living condition, we need food in the fridge and in the cabinets, we need to pay rent on time before housing takes our shelter, we need clothing for the seasons' elements, it can't be the same ensemble for winters and summers, instead of relying on help from others we need something we can count on like a bank account. I'm going to ride with the hustlers and killas to raise figures, so our banco can be popular, I'm going to replace the wealth of my deceased bread-winning, illegal-earning father. I can no longer see you crying, struggling and suffering, you tried to hide it but I always saw the make-up running, my body used to quiver watching you shiver. I love you and I know you love me but I'm going to sacrifice myself for money.

I'm roaming the streets with packs and heat cutting throats as I walked the beat, ogs used to warn me but that same day the next day and days after, I'm walking around advertising and bumping my color, they knew me since I was a kid and know my story, they knew I was hungry and weren't going to stop me, so they told me "start your own spizzy, shorty". So, I did it, I stood in the park on my side like if I was stationary, smokers that wanted quality searched till they found me. From a hustling nomad, I went to pitchn on one of the most lucrative puntos in the hill.

Albert 'Infinite the Poet' Carrasco

I was a preteen, getting cream, living out momma's nightmares and my dreams, I started with packs of different color caps from different bosses of traps to my own purée being weighed on triple beams.

In a few months, I had a squadron of young hungry brothers with me that lived in that same apartment building hustling, it was the early eighties, there was enough money for everybody, we all had a position to maintain, the bellaco crew became the team's name, by the late eighties we were all infamous in the street life hall of fame for the cooked cocaine game. Our crack block was moving like hunts point, Watson, the blvd and 138 street dope spots. Everybody except our parents was happy about the generated currency, we're flashing wads of cash, wearing name brand threads and thousands in jewelry, driving whips back-to-back on the ave, throwing up the peace sign every time we passed. We did it . . . that's what we yelled as we said "salud", tapping bottles of champagne while smiling and laughing.

By ninety-one, two succumbed to the gun. Now, we're feeling pain from ill-gotten gains while mothers filled with sorrow that'll never see their children tomorrow dripped tear drops on the windowpane. We weren't prepared for death, we were preparing for success and not to regress.

What do you tell parents when they told us over and over the apparent? Sorry? Oops, my bad? Nothing can replace what comes after the rupture of a mother's water bag, nothing can replace a child to a proud dad, so after death, I stood silent next to family members mourning on those deadly days and nights, especially on the third day in a church before burial at nine thirty in the morning. I stood quiet but inside anger was inciting a riot.

It was all good on the come up to be heirs until we got to a level where death was now in the air.

We weren't scared, we lived in hell, why would we be? By the new millennium, a gang off peers turned to a posse, from a posse we went to clique, from a clique to a few good men, feeling the repercussions of bad but necessary decisions. There's a few of us in the street, the rest rests in cemeteries or sleep imprisoned.

Judgment Day

Next up . . . Mr. Carrasco . . . Scared to death, I approach. I hear my life being narrated before me.

Drugs, guns, violence, pestilence . . . I am now frightened! My judgment was about to be chosen.

Wait . . . wait one minute! Yes, I did everything you said I did but I've learnt from it, and I teach what was taught to me by the devil but as a righteous man. My judgment paused. All eyes are on me. I beg your pardon! I was born a pure soul, circumstances and my environment took its toll.

You know the strength of temptation and the power of evil, if there was no satan, I wouldn't be questioned and then condemned from entering heaven. While roaming hell's surface, I frequently called onto you for direction and guidance out of violence and deception, I didn't want to do wrong, I wanted to do right, but I was lied to. I didn't see light; I saw flames at both ends of the tunnel. I heard the devil serenade daily, I had the heart and tools of his trade, he wanted me to make the fat girl sing but both death tunes I had the power to evade.

He didn't like that. He couldn't control me, I didn't sell my soul so he didn't own me, but for quite some time he did persuade me to work for him as a way out of poverty. I was hell's waiter while I was pitchn to those that signed hell's waiver and entered Hell's Kitchen. I lost three decades of my life waiting on a sign from you, I lost almost every member of my crew and when those doves flew, I cried, I looked up to the sky watching those doves fly till the sun burnt my eyes, hoping that when they reach you, they can make it through too.

Before it's a yay or nay, I have a bit more to say . . . I turned around, I left the devil alone on my own, I wasn't threatened nor scared, I just got tired of thinking of and physically looking at all the scars I bare. I got tired of running nowhere ever so quickly, so I just stopped abruptly. Not only did I stop, after a ten-year search of finding the infinite within, I returned to the streets like a teacher off sabbatical to teach my kin and to uplift my kin with wise words being spoken.

I got people to put their guns down, put the coke and dope down, I'm educating men, women and children, I took away but I'm giving back to citizens. Before today, my face was faith to those that lived blasphemous. I want to get into heaven, can I please be forgiven for my previous life of living scandalously? The angels heard my plea, it started to rain, they cried for me. That's when I heard . . . "son, follow me".

Albert 'Infinite the Poet' Carrasco

Man, Near Death, and His Guardian Angel

They cried holding each other.
They tried to comfort each other.
They overstood each other.
Only if they could temporarily switch.
One will get to go where the other is at in the future.
One was where, the other was in the past and can never return.
They cry for the same reason.
Loved ones.
I just want to feel the love that was lost . . .
So do I.
They could tell each other about family.
He / she is good,
I see 'em daily.
One can see what the other can't and vice versa . . .
Can you please explain how I feel about them to them?
Most certainly. May I ask that you do the same for me?
I promise.
Okay, I'm going to be amongst those standing vigil.
Get back in your physical.
I'll never leave your side . . .
We have a heartbeat!!!!!

Ahead of My Time... from the Streets to the Stages

A Gallery of Pictures

Ahead of My Time . . . from the Streets to the Stages

Albert 'Infinite the Poet' Carrasco

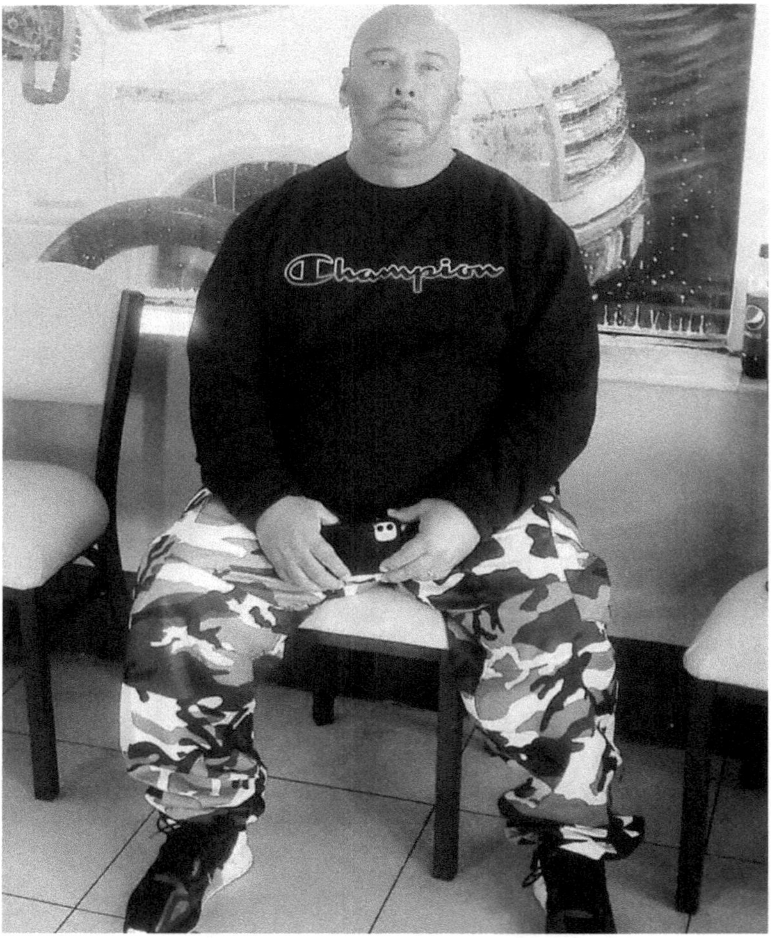

Ahead of My Time . . . from the Streets to the Stages

Albert 'Infinite the Poet' Carrasco

Ahead of My Time... from the Streets to the Stages

Albert 'Infinite the Poet' Carrasco

Ahead of My Time . . . from the Streets to the Stages

Albert 'Infinite the Poet' Carrasco

Albert 'Infinite the Poet' Carrasco

Ahead of My Time . . . from the Streets to the Stages

Albert 'Infinite the Poet' Carrasco

Ahead of My Time . . . from the Streets to the Stages

Albert 'Infinite the Poet' Carrasco

Ahead of My Time... from the Streets to the Stages

Albert 'Infinite the Poet' Carrasco

Albert 'Infinite the Poet' Carrasco

epilogue

about the Author...

Albert Carrasco, AKA **Infinite the Poet**, AKA **Infinite**, is an urban poet, mentor and public speaker.

Infinite the Poet grew up in the east part of the Bronx and still resides there; so, he knows many young men will follow the same dark path he followed looking for change. The life of crime should never be an option to being poor, but it is very often so.

Infinite believes his experience of growing up in poverty, dealing with drugs and witnessing murder over and over were lessons learnt, in order to gain knowledge to teach. His harsh reality and honesty are a powerfully packed punch, delivered through rhyme.

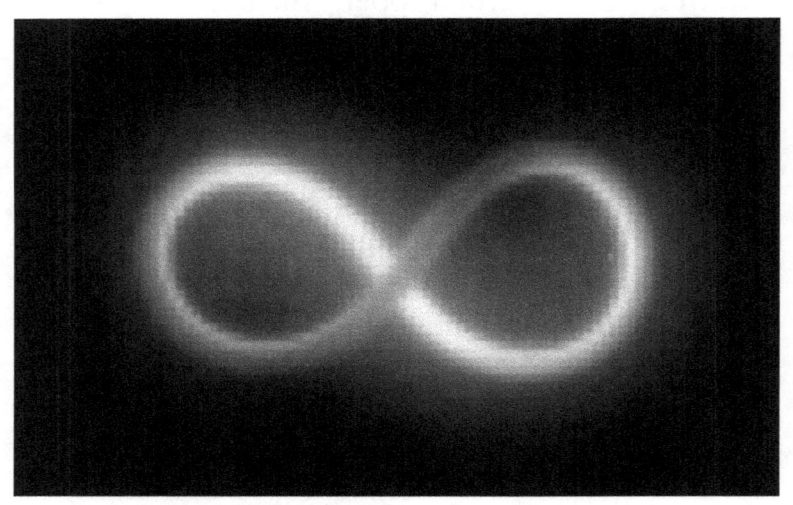

Infinite the Poet

Infinite The Poet's

Web Links

Infinite poetry @lulu.com

Alcarrasco2 on YouTube

Infinite the poet on reverbnation
Infinite Poetry

http://www.lulu.com/us/en/shop/al-infinite-carrasco/infinite-poetry/paperback/product-21040240.html

www.facebook.com/alcarrasco2

Inner Child Press

Inner Child Press is a publishing company founded and operated by writers. Our personal publishing experiences provide us an intimate understanding of the sometimes-daunting challenges writers, new and seasoned may face in the business of publishing and marketing their creative "Written Work".

For more information:

Inner Child Press

www.innerchildpress.com

intouch@innerchildpress.com

'building bridges of cultural understanding'
202 Wiltree Court, State College, Pennsylvania 16801

www.ingramcontent.com/pod-product-compliance
Lightning Source LLC
Chambersburg PA
CBHW070547160426
43199CB00014B/2402